# The Live Science of the Elements

\*

essay

\*

# Traumear

Paperback ISBN  978-0-244-82595-9


*


www.traumear.com

*

These live sciences, like the present one, are works of transition from development to evolution. When a human being evolves he has to cope with the fact that 'everything changes', even the meaning of 'everything' and of 'change'. How he goes about this, necessarily with the help of the spirit of truth, depends on his constitution and on his gifts or talents – in other words on what he brought with him into the world at his birth. Of course he must discover – and it will partly be revealed to him – how he is to work and what kind of work he is to do during his evolution. He is to die to the old world and to build up his endless world. Works which arise from such initial evolutionary impulses and processes, such these live sciences like the present, will then stimulate and facilitate the transition in some others who are ready to evolve.

*

# The Live Science of the Elements

All the elements together make up the stuff of the universe. They are either arranged or disturbed. In the order of the universe the elements are arranged in a pattern. This pattern has been discussed in our philosophy. It pervades throughout all the distributions and configurations of elementary reality, and may be detected or implicated in everything which depends on shape or form. The totality of the elementary stuff of the universe however is not patterned. Some of it always remains in chaos, and as such it is said to be elemental. Chaos, or chaotic stuff, does not exist in time. Neither of course does it exist then in eternity. But it does exist. Or, to be more precise, it may exist. It cannot exist under any given conditions. This makes it clear that we do not mean that it may exist if, but that it may exist period.

The difference between elementary reality and elemental chaos then is the pattern. It is an eightfold pattern, which means that it unfolds itself in eight different ways. This does not imply that something fivefold unfolds itself in five different ways, or that something twofold unfolds itself in two different ways. It is inherent in the number eight that the universal pattern of elements may unfold itself. This will become more clear when we deal with the science of numbers. The pattern itself is nothing aside of the universal impression of order. When it is expressed – which is the same, in this case, as to say 'when it expresses itself' – since this pattern is the only thing in the universe in which impression and expression coincide – when it is expressed or expresses itself it leads to elementary processes, eight in number. These processes are all unique among processes, because they are uncaused. They are also peculiar in their own right, because they are not essential. This means that a total expression of the elementary pattern is purely effective and existential. Pure effect is not followed by cause, and 'exis-

1

tential' refers to a state which is not succeeded by essence. Since effect and cause is a physical relation, and since existence and essence is a mental relation, and is implied therefore in the physical, we may deduce that every expression of the elementary pattern is a habit.

Chaos never exists except nevertheless. It is the last bit of swamp which is drained off. While it participates in time it is given another name, such as disorder, turmoil and anarchy. It is interesting to note that all manner of chaos which may exist in the world cannot possibly exist in nature or in reality. This allow us to induce, in fact it almost demands and dictates that we induce, the human origin of all chaos. This chaos is the child of man. Without it, granted, we might possibly be able to exist, although there is no guarantee. With it however, and in its abounding presence, we have both opportunity and occasion to show what stuff we are made of. It presents to us, as a fact, the bitter edge of final judgment. Oh, this is no great joy to think about. But only do it and see! you will gain the priceless possession of omnipotence over yourself, which is called self-mastery. This is a different thing from self-control and from self-knowledge. Self-knowledge was raised to its limit of inconsequence by the early Greeks, in particular by Socrates, who purportedly did choose not to evade the world's reply to his suggestion. Self-control on the other hand was developed by the early Jews to its eventual result of pointlessness, and it was practiced with special insight by their scribes and Pharisees, and with particular emphasis by Caiaphas the High Priest, who is reported to have encouraged injustice for the sake of universal integrity, which is a fine sentiment, is it not? The greater Romans of the day practiced a hybrid combination of self-control and self-knowledge, which we call self-analysis. It may lead to self-syntheses, but if it does, that is a fortunate accident. The chance of it happening is zero. Self-analysis is always fatalistic, and fatalism is the specialty of the Moslems.

2

Their self-analysis achieves literal perfection. The Koran is a statement of qualified faith. Such a thing will either amuse or it must deject. Prime samples of both moode may be found in Arabia. The Jewish sentiment on the other hand will always attempt to rule the outside world. That is the essence of good humour unless one holds it up to the truth, in which case it turns into the essence of tragedy. Eventually it must be held up to the truth, and then it will be divided into death and legitimate sentimentality. The latter will then be viewed as the religion of the world, and it will be tantamount to actual beauty. In the meantime the Jewish people insist on good luck.

The impact of self-analysis on the world has brought about, by reaction, something called Roman law. It is the public demonstration of the philosophic non-sequitur. But the outcome of this reaction is the aspect of the Catholic Church. It is supremely and definitively synthetic. The mighty structure of this Church can not be overrated, because it includes even the appearances of time. These are elemental. No other church has done this, which amounts to a logical conquest of temporality, for the sake of the world's complete instruction. The extent of the achievement is liable to make us swoon. Contemporary growth of the Catholic Church reflects the fruit of those labours. Peter has without a doubt overcome his tendency to vacillate and he rests secure in the constancy of his convictions. His final conviction, the corner-stone of his morality so to speak, may be understood in terms of lay approval. His humility towers above the conceivable. When the shepherd gives his life, not for the flock, but for the single lost sheep, he rises to unpremeditatable heights. From there he will for the first time view reality, which until then he has only conceived. He will comprehend the necessity of his previous limitation, and the fruit of those limitations he will harvest in due time. It is a consequence of his firmness and of his magnanimity.

*

3

There is no such thing as one single element. We may speak of a particular element however, as though it did exist, when in fact it only would. Once conditioned, it is not any more an element. While it plainly exists on the other hand it cannot be differentiated from other elements as a particular thing. Consequently we speak of an element as that bit of universal stuff which would exist if it could. As such it contains an intensity. This intensity is of no use whatsoever unless it is mastered. If it is mastered it is transferable, and then it becomes a most potent carrier of energy. The energy transferred by the mastered intensity of an element is so powerful that nothing on earth can withstand it. The effect of such an elementary act is the utter separation of that to which the energy is transferred into the worthy and the impotent, and the destruction of the latter by the former. Elementary acts are possible only since the event of the world's end, since even the possibility of resistance to the element's intensity must be absent if the intensity is to be mastered. There must be a perfect concentration of the sense apparatus if the transfer is to come about, so that neither resentment nor hasty judgment on one hand, and neither ill will nor false passion on the other hand, inhibit the perfect progress of change, as intense energy is brought to bear. If this energy is converted into strength, as it must be unless it is to be wasted, it becomes absolute strength, which does not depend upon any systematic application, whether the system be psychosomatic, logical or solar, and which is not limited by any mental or bodily function, whether this function be, or pertain to, instinct, intellect, intuition or intelligence, but it springs spontaneously from the flesh and arises impulsively from the soul, one or the other, depending upon the nature of the opportunity, whether it is initial or responsive.

Elements cannot be given names. They are in themselves nominal. Therefore they may be observed. The reason for such observation is the embodiment of elements as strictly human entities. Their observation must be endless, meaning that it does not terminate in the thing observed. Since elements cannot be broken down, a subtlety of approach is required, propitious to the particular state in which they find themselves. These states give proof of the elements, and one takes advantage of this in order to expose the elements to the senses by provoking their appearance. While the elements are still instated we must know that they impose upon us, so that we are ignorantly burdened or stupidly depressed. The provocation proceeds periodically. Instinct is of the essence. Care prevents it from becoming undue. Eventually, after some persistence, the element leaps from its state and into order. Subsequently one is not aware of it as such.

If we envision the state of the element, we find that it is remarkable. Once remarked, it is susceptible to abstraction. One merely appends to the element, for the duration of the time, a significant point of reference while abstraction takes place, and finally the element is sorted out. The point of reference is then simply effaced. Vision allows for the ordering of the element on account of its own source, which is immeasurable.

Elements can also be ejected from their state. What is required here is both the wish to do so and a capacity of power. The latter is arranged by dint of power reflection. The capacitating of the element automatically follows suit. Its state is electrically deflected for a time so that the element is able to emit a charge. A moment of deflation sets in, which leaves room for the application of force, so that the element gains momentum. This alone suffices, since order is present, and the element is literally taken over by this presence of order, supplied by the fulfilment of the wish. The instigation of this entire process of element ejection has to be environmentally effected however, and we only bring it about by establishing the elemental cause. Once established it does for all time.

All the elements are finally part and parcel of human nature. This is when peace is universal. So that this peace can never again be interrupted it is rooted in the soul. Now the soul is all-powerful. Its present effectiveness transcends even those merely outward appearances which have for so long presented a problem to the creative imagination. Materially impenetrable phenomena are mechanically transformed and reinstated in the cosmic order of things as the shape of contemplation. All of our impulses are now innately understood and the mystery of creation stands revealed here in the light of day.

The elements ca now be viewed in terms of each other. This gives rise to an element picture. It may be intuited. In the light of reason it takes on appearance. We find ourselves face to face with the inchoation of beauty. The senses at first find it difficult to cope with this experience. Concentration seems arduous and our power of reflection seems disinclined to come into operation. The sheer habit of perseverance allows the senses a period of intensity so as to rise to the occasion. By inchoation we mean free genesis, which is to say coming into creation in terms of itself. Conceived as a process, inchoation reveals both its effect and the fact that this effect is caused while the cause is not available or accessible. The experience of this process therefore seems to invite perceptual isolation which makes itself felt as a kind of trance or spell. The brain however contradicts this isolation by rendering the body immune to it. Hence the process is caused to lead to an issue. This issue in the present case is beauty. For the first time we are able to witness the original presence of beauty itself.

The elements can also be known in relation to each other. This is where intuitive contemplation is of the essence. An elementary shape is brought into existence. It materializes upon recognition by the brain. Consequently it takes place. The mind creates for it a fitting locality and here it gains the required form and the proper content.

In relation to each other the elements are constantly in motion. Between any two elements a polarity is set up which may be analyzed. Due to the polarity one may speak of a distance between the two participant elements, and as this distance increases, radiation occurs. A description of this phenomenon suffices at the moment. Radiation has magnitude in its own right, prior to any particular manifestation of itself. The polarity in which any two elements participate may be entailed or intense. In the case of intense polarity, radiation is atmospheric, meaning that it manifests itself in terms of unlimited gravity. Gravity and radiation as we know are cosmic counterparts. In the case of entailed polarity, radiation transcends and in turn we have aesthetic magnitude. This is a phenomenon which instils all phenomena within the single effect of beauty.

The various elements of any particular thing eventually take effect on one another and we are brought face to face with one definitive aspect of human reality. The result is a magnificent experience. Our entire being is uplifted to a plane of universal insight and of cosmic understanding. We are well aware of what this means in terms of our future living. The future as such is brought into a tangible context with us and our own future begins to assert itself in terms of the eternal game of life. All that is future is presently decided upon a substantial basis which may be analyzed to reveal elementary consistency and consequence. Let us for example examine the vision of our personal future. It occurs to us in terms of the flesh and with respect to the earth. At first there seems to be no opportunity for perception even though the images are doubtless and steady. As time accumulates however, measure upon measure of visional substance is acquired and processed while the imagination is pondered. Distinct relationships are referred to thought and reason affords them form and shape. It is important to understand that all impressions are somehow relevant and that our exposure to them suffices to give them credibility and familiarity.

For we know that our future establishes us at our origin and that whatever we become is what we were.

All the elements that go into a particular composition of eternal magnitude occur either objectively or subjectively to the faculty of intelligence which maintains them for the sake of their duration. Given the required scope of productivity and the appropriate natural circumstance, these elements stream out into the field of vision. Here they may easily be perceived. Since it is impossible to perceive one of them at a time, one concentrates rather on what is called the elemental picture, which is open to scrutiny and may be grasped by the intellect.

This elemental picture is of great interest. We study it patiently and are soon able to take it in as a whole. There seems to be no division of parts at all, even though we know that it is made up of parts, and this leads us to assume at least a superficial fusion of parts. In response we are faced with the generation of positive absolute activity. The attributes of this activity are royalty and mastery. We go back to the picture. Now we discover a twofold representative quality, which we call texture and text. It has all the earmarks of a content-form relationship, but this cannot be the case, for the experience of the picture is presently substantial. Hence we look to our understanding for a possible explanation. The absolute activity mentioned above manifests itself eminently, as new matter. We do not mean new with respect to old, but in terms of itself. Eminent manifestation is not open to experience and is not to be tested. New matter cannot be broken down and cannot be analyzed. We say that it has environmental stability. Once it has begun to participate in sensation it may be referred to as live matter. A distinction between objectivity and subjectivity is not any more relevant.

Live matter may be contemplated as the shape of peace. The essence of its being, its humanity, does not vacillate with temporary variation, but remains constant. We imbibe this constancy both by instinct and through the nerves. It is in fact the diet of our nerves and the stuff which makes them up. Our nerves are the life-centres of our flesh. They concentrate light for the sake of its embodiment. We picture them as a network for the transport of stimuli and for the carrying of impulses, but such a picture does not even entail their substantial purpose, which can only be envisioned. Ultimately this purpose is the immediate incarnation of all of our experience.

Live matter has fixed energy. Since it has this energy, rather than containing or possessing it, there is no difficulty in simply extracting it through use, and of course it is only in use that fixed energy can be suitably defined. It is said to be fixed because it is self-conditioned, so that it requires no application, and because its presence and sense are one, so that it is neither sought out nor experienced, but it is simply here. Its description is radioactivity. This means that its power and its effectiveness are absolutely distinct, and that concrete materiality is wholly open to it. Radioactivity is cosmically bound. It infects the flesh insofar as the flesh is beneficially established, causing it to emanate from beauty. Beauty consequently becomes a distinct source of carnal pleasure. If the flesh on the other hand is still to any degree mortal, this radioactivity behaves as an infestation, causing the emancipation of all being in terms of that flesh. The issue of such an emancipation is true enthusiasm, which is of the soul.

Fixed energy gives rise to what we call right strength. Strength is right as it goes into this action, into the act of the present moment, and it is wholly there. No distinction is made between effort and achievement, between purpose and end, but the strength invested is in fact the strength gained. We can understand what right strength is only when we know that strength in itself is good. In the case of right strength it is not required to wait for an alien or hostile impulse or for some strange influence according to which strength might align itself but while the result is contemplated, during the performing of an activity, or in the face of some planned behaviour, a surfeit of strength is held in readiness, while we are in possession of it, and in terms of it the particular creation goes on. Right strength is always intentional and explicit.

Fixed energy is the basis of open power. We say that power is open when it establishes itself anew and grows spontaneously even as it goes into operation and during its implementation. The particular dispensation of open power goes on presently and helps to illustrate the plan of the truth. This plan is consequently open to the outward senses. Open power is effective for the installation in of special attributes. It consciousness shows and carries that particular aspect of the truth which imbues final definition in accordance with original intent. The personality cannot offer any inhibition and character can only give aid, while reason is embodied wherever this power establishes itself. The embodiment of reason is in fact new talent in progress. Such talent has neither potential nor capacity, but it works itself out under motivations inherent in itself, and it is not surmised but live experience. We can evoke this open power in ourselves and we can invoke it in each other, not for an purpose or application in mind, but for the sake of its own resourceful enjoyment. Such an enjoyment of this power, resourceful in any way that we see fit, fills us with regal satisfaction, so that our feelings, emotions and passions, and even our sentiments, may be expressly described in terms of themselves and each other, and not at the risk of their diminishment but with the result of their enrichment.

Open power and right strength lead to capital action. This is action which sets forth, in general and particular terms at once, the final meaning of humanity. It is action which stems from the head, originates in the heart, and starts from the soul. It is the case of humanity acting itself out. With reference to the human being as such, capital action may be described as the establishment of man. In terms of itself it is viewed as the final work. Reaction to it is not possible, for its process is automatic and its motivation mechanical. Its undertaking implies the pure reliance upon substance. There can be no question of applicability or appropriateness since its cause and effect are one. With respect to the imagination it is made up purely and simply of the light of day. A manipulation of live matter universally presented: this is how it may be defined. Its result can be measured in the name of peace, bliss, and glory. But no man lives who has not at least had a dream of this. Whatever happens to be true today sets off this action in us and we respond with pleasure. The special oneness of what happens with this action of ours is sublime happiness and cannot be surpassed.

Finally we come to live substance. It is its own cause. Indeed it may be described as pure causality. All that is alive is given and may be taken for granted in terms of this substance, and it means instantaneous life. No analysis of life can go beyond it, and if it goes so far it is rewarded conclusively. The various parts of the human body are introduced to this substance and given over to it until our whole body is its lively and quickening example. Our mind is transformed in such a way and in such a manner that live substance takes its place and holds it in motion. Our soul is brought up into it so that it relates as live substance. This means that we communicate with absolute ease. Our flesh is turned into carrier, means and birth of live substance.

So that live substance may be one with itself it is introduced to the world, and the world, insofar as it is made, is made for that reason.

This world we speak of is in fact made up of all the elements that are humanly conceivable. Let us therefore conceive those elements so that we may recognize the world and become capable of recognition within it.

Within the world all power is firmly fixed. We do not, and indeed should not hope to, come across any instances or examples of power, such as might vindicate our existence or in any way establish ourselves as independent units of life. Instead we realize that this fixed power begins and ends with those human faculties that have become, so to speak, safe and sound. They may neither be corrupted from within nor damaged from without, pertaining, consequently, with respect to human progress, to finished business. The power that is available in our world, in other words, is gained purely in line with our application of ourselves to it wherever we may find it. The application in turn is equal in strength to the intensity of the available power; that this is so cannot be helped but may be both understood and loved.

So that there be no conflict between understanding and love, nor even between the love of understanding and the understanding of love, that same world is made beautiful. Its beauty compensates. Over and against this beauty we establish our constant willingness. Above and beyond this establishment the world's beauty stimulates the emergence of our own beauty which in turn furthers the beauty of the world. We do in fact beautify the world not by any effort of achievement but solely by our habit of authentic and specific living. The effect of this habit is omnipotent.

The beauty of the world is believed in order to be seen. We might also say that it is evoked for the sake of its perception. Each and every such act of belief or work of evocation gives rise to a distinct creation, or creature, of beauty that may be accounted for in terms of the world and solicited on its behalf. For it is certainly to our advantage that the world is made as quickly and as soon as possible, and it lies in our interest to beget the world as early as we may.

The world is always at least matter or material. To this corresponds our desire for form and our longing for shape. The desire and the longing approach the world as matter or material while at the same time the world, as matter or material, approaches our perception. At the moment of inception reason occurs. Why this is so, and how this happens, is really not very interesting, but that it happens, and that it cannot be otherwise, is important indeed. It is because of reason and due to reason that the world is human. Our awareness of this gives unfailing proof.

Once we have reason in the world we are both finally and eternally free. This freedom is turned, by our action, into the world's recognizable pattern, and this pattern is of value. By means of it we appreciate the world. The pattern itself is like the material appearance of or body, and since the two are alike, this pattern and this appearance, they may at any time be reproductively interchanged. They are spectral phenomena. Principally they serve as factors of limitation, protecting, guarding, and finally sealing, so that nothing may ever disturb, interrupt or shake the world, but it is without end.

*

What we do when we observe ourselves, in the traditional balance between love and security, allows for a description well worth the effort, for it arranges before our gaze an element of life too tranquil to be tested by ordinary means and not accessible to the usual experimental functioning of this intellect of ours. We have forgotten, perhaps, the discrepancy in logic that accompanies every organism on its venture from beginning to end, from alpha to omega. The pedestrian task of suitably designating cycles of the kind falls to those who often leave themselves open to the charge of having disturbed that very balance, that delicate poise, created steadfastly in the heart and upheld by the intent mind, even while our humanity fails and falters. Strength has its uses while no other experience changes its guise favourably enough for us to participate in that change. Strength loosens the bonds for us when all else fails. A particular matter comes to our attention and we let it drop because we lack the stimulation. The temporal physiognomy, the bone structure of dead things brought to life again, preposterous except for the few, overshadows, from one standard appreciation to the next, what our senses have informed, what our betters have instructed. Therefore it lies heavily on our conscience that so many upbraid each other for no reason, that a cold light illuminates all being for them who are too busy with the stereotype, too much stretched on the wheel of fortune to respond to the neglected will.

Strength supplies us with an eagerness too radiant to be catchy. The mind probes faithfully; one ascertains as much. So far as our work is concerned, we seem to lack limitation on the side of profit and advantage, while on the side of appearances we lack cunning and subterfuge. But this should be taken as a visible commendation of our behaviour in the light of very basic and fundamental changes, changes that leave us little room, if any, for developing a manner, a style, or a category of belief.

We estimate the duration of elementary processes in terms of struggle and with regard to upheavals, great or small, so that a unity of mastered impulses may be achieved and a oneness of intelligence attributed. A test case may be isolated for the sake of illustration. Whatever sensation leads us out of a closed system of deed and observance may also contain within it, like a seed, the next actual stimulant on which the established open work would depend. The conditional reflex is disregarded. We stop ourselves somewhere along the line of what has all the appearances of a trial and while we avoid any excesses, such as overindulgences in felt stuff, we correct all tendencies to the contrary of our self-imposed momentum towards an as yet unknown relativity of being. If the strain becomes a problem, we do not hasten to remove the strain but we accept the problem, interpret it along the lines of our original course and carry the solution out. The very nature of an elementary solution always remains subtle, but must never be allowed to remain vague. It is incumbent upon us as conscientious upholders of open states of mind, to treat all management of fixed emotion as a preamble; neither to exploit nor to discard, but to emphasize, perhaps, for the sake of edification, and then unfailingly to attract or to direct, depending at that time on our own attraction or direction. For we attract the elements, as extension of the substance we were and will be, and we direct them in line and on a par with the substance we are. Are we not substantial? And are we not substantial ever more? Then the elements leave us no recourse until we include them, draw them here with us, lend them our own purpose and even make it over to them, finally, oh happy thought!

The elementary vision proclaims itself for our utter absorption into it, trusting our unconditional and re-established freedom, and we connect factions here, construct illusions there, propose immanent expediency everywhere, and we hold out gamely before the universal laughter: it cannot touch us because it is not meant for us, but to recoil upon its own source.

Associate with this vision, even as the heart inclines, disturbances of mind, physical abasements, shortcomings before lofty flights of sense. Perform the association if it helps. Annex the intrusion that would claim prior reference, no matter how exalted. Sanction only, in these spheres, the agreement with the vision itself. But then such an agreement requires no further sanctioning.

There is a simple, short way of putting it: as the vision goes on, the elements come too. One develops an appetite for them and welcomes their transfusion. No haphazard appeal to a particle of sense in us can go unchallenged, and more often than not – go intrinsically unchallenged. Our high calling would have it so. We should keep this in mind.

As a just proposal of nature personified, this tendency in man to create himself an external substance runs counter to the vision of elements in reality put to use. Hence the apparent clash with the extinct modus vivendi. Hence, also, the running conflict out there involving matter and its extensions, on a level none of us seem to be able to agree upon.

Outwardly, then, we distinguish between what happens, whether or not it fits in with our own plans for creation, and what can be broken down into particles of resistance too numerous to count, but accountable nevertheless not for what happens – this is the crux of the matter – but for what we make of it. The positioning of these two elements can not be overstressed. It had long become a bad habit to connect in our minds, after a fashion unsupportable except on the basis of more such bad habits, what in reality stands distinguished for a very good reason, and that is to offer us means and example, so that we might become real ourselves. But when means and example are misread as cause and effect, as essence and existence, as form and content, to mention only three such mistakes, and their connection in our mind as finished out there is allowed to rule persuasively over our faculties, these faculties must soon be rendered incapable of furthering anything but their own undignified collapse.

What happens out there, then, we have called the example, and this, as the element understood presently, affords us both a point of departure and a way of return.

Whatever can be broken down into particles of resistance out there we have called a means, and it is this property, not of disintegration, as some seem to suppose, but of total divisibility, that places into our hands the optimum creative tool.

The example as a point of departure emphatically prepares us, as experimental beings, for inner growth and for the dissolution of all hindrances to that growth. We may even go so far as to concentrate on a detail of the example, if we wish to ascertain the full fruition, eventually, of our most internal being. As the example absorbs our perception, we do not insist on a perceptual parallel somewhere, instigated, as it would have to be, by an idolatrous motivation, nor do we persist in perceiving once the perceptual sample has gone, but we empty ourselves responsively, adding nothing to the given experience and taking nothing away from it. This emptiness is then illuminated from within so that the sample may return in order. We must let go of what we wish to know so that we may know it in fact. For the fact of our knowledge is inward, and inwardly left, where we cannot observe it, not outwardly held.

As a way of return, the example would at first elude us, if indeed we held it as an idea or as a named concept. Simply expected, however, and not in line with any particular mode of experience, it presents itself in time and profitably limits our perception. Such a limit moves us. This will seem contrary to extinct experience, where limits only coincided with a stop to things. The moving limit, as an outcome of exemplary experience, leaves us in no doubt as to the relevant progress of our being. Whether transitive or intransitive, it carries within it, as part and parcel of its original make-up, what can only be described as an electric charge. For us, therefore, receptivity is of the essence, and a docile passivity of the rational will. We undertake only the casual remnant of the experience, while we remain conscious of our role during and throughout the approach. Except for interruptions of a superior kind, where our attention is redrawn, nothing may sway us from our purpose, which is lofty or aloof. An exaggeration helps at times. Aggravations, on the other hand, are to be ignored. A gentle pressure, exerted at the right moment, perhaps sexually motivated, can be of use, as a furtherance of our ultimate interest.

The property of total divisibility, which we have called a means, lasts while a habit is being made of it. Subject and object should not be viewed as separate here. It lasts while that which divides is being divided. It may be viewed as a thing in itself or an instrumental property, and in both cases we do well to take any interest in the logical conclusions that may be drawn from the sheer fact of such a property.

To divide means principally to ascertain energy and to locate both source and end of that energy. A partial division, such as when a choice of matter is involved, always determines a particular end, but incompletely, and the source it reveals cannot fully impart itself to our senses; there always remains an illusion of coarse matter. However a total division leaves no remnant, so that energy is distributed not only piecemeal, qualitatively, but also, and mainly, quantitatively, and we may say that it leaves no tracks. Its path may be surmised. The end of quantities of energy really locates itself, after the sure knowledge that we have of our own origin and of the things that pertain to it. So too with the source of these quanta; it shows itself even as we find it, and no superior cause may be premeditated.

If we look now to the applications of this ascertained energy, we arrive at an institution, and principally at a live institution. The distribution of energy quanta pertains only to what we hear and see and feel first hand and never to ideas, to ideals, to theories or hypotheses, to mental pictures or image constructs. It relates to those who worship with their eyes open. And, we might add parenthetically, it destroys those who worship their open eyes.

Live institution actuates an increment of substance out here.

The perfect encounter with energy in quantity releases into the world patterns of behaviour, and these patterns automatically take the time and place of conduct on a basis. But since conduct on a basis also implies an illiberality of motive, such as various safeguards and diverse insurances, we may take for granted that these patterns of behaviour are freely concrete. To think of them even as bound by their own definition is to introduce a falsehood and to prevent to that degree the proliferation of such patterns.

We comprehend these patterns then not as isolated instances, but as behaviour on the whole, ruled with respect, accurate in relation and suitable in terms. Whatever occasion is given us to work such a pattern into another sphere of reference should not be seen as less of a distinction but as an opportunity to help build the world.

Every increment of substance out here delivers us to a degree from the containment of our own selfish aspirations. We do well, therefore, to immerse as much of our being as we can in the faultless being of him whose nature purifies our own by permitting his total division that we may exalt his name. The world we build he has planned for us. The world we make he prepared for us. The world we institute he presents to us. Therefore none of us need concern ourselves with a comparison for our works or a justification for our deeds or a testimony to our being. One might say that our existences overlap. This is no haphazard solution to a historical problem but now, at this moment, as you look and see, destiny overwhelms itself and our simple wishes come true.

*

An explicit use can be made of the elements when we choose them intelligently. For this we must learn to recognize them, as symptoms of power, initially, and then, against a backdrop of cold fact, as points of glory.

By points of glory we mean nothing that cannot be figured, though initially they lend themselves only to recognition pure and simple. What it principally amounts to is a position that might be identified but it locates, for the energetic brain, a subliminal reference instead, and this is where a long memory comes into its own. One observes, and perhaps one observes enthusiastically, but denies oneself the identification. While the moment lasts, so does our concentration. Each note of recognition is captured as on a ruled field, favoured by one premise or another, tested and then trained. The backdrop of cold fact that we mentioned serves as a guide, a formidable support system, previously collated and analytically sound to the point of exceeding permanence.

Out of it springs – or rises, depending on whether one's mind espouses trend or ambivalence – the disposed contact. It needs no further introduction, especially not to the source of intelligence on which our own feeds, as a babe on its mother's breast. The cast of the backdrop, the set of the field, the mainspring of energetic recognition: as specified by these three an expression of reality comes to the fore. Once again we must remind ourselves that the cause and effect relationship must actively be avoided as extinct when- and wherever it would still claim a remnant of thought. – An organic expression of reality would not be better, but simply good. We search out instances of necessity, we supply right strength, exact action, even as outward parameters where required, and finally an association or a preamble to something seems to trigger off the correct procedure, the fitting process or the fine way.

This fine way affords us splendid vistas of our actual life and of its meaning both inward and outward. These vistas centre our experience for us and cement it in beauty. Shock cannot dislocate this centrality but only make it firm and solid. One explores here the kind of attractive resistance that is called earth and with some wise management that resistance gives in to our moods, leaving beauty playfully displayed. We now call it glory and it forbids our abuse of it. Its richness either draws us or leaves us floundering. We shall not dismiss any of our faculties now, or consider degrees of worthiness, since that, at least, has been decided, besides, at any rate, being beyond us; nevertheless some are pushed back. There are those who come to this and deplore it, for their memory lacks zeal. Others would force themselves past it, through it, and their vision is stopped.

*

Also we may know the elements, formerly having chosen them, as modes of investment for our greater comprehension of what we love.

The sentimental love of these chosen elements may cause us harm only with overindulgence, or with the taking of an unfair advantage where generosity is possible. A zealous spirit often apprehends the catastrophic end.

To know the elements means to labour towards their institution as ends.

Knowledge of the elements presupposes a safe familiarity with bare matter and comic stuff.

Known elements escape from the surrounding flux of bare matter in order to seek distribution as befits their nature.

Where elements, due to our knowing influence, are expelled from various extinct perceptual complexes, and where we manage to prevent them from becoming fixed again, due to a casual perseverance, they create for themselves an aura of distinction by which they may be recognized in future. There are elements for example, which may be categorically referred to their steadfastness as moments of visible light. We may then appreciate this visible light by relying on our ability eventually to align these concerted elements according to the necessity of the moment.

An element series has special application from the point of view we develop while under the influence of cosmic stuff. An element series, therefore, protects, primarily, during total relative exposure, and secondarily it leads out of any occlusion of bare matter where otherwise we might run the risk of a serious progress postponement.

An element series serves as the model for organic series of any sort or kind, and it pays us to study it as a phenomenon, both under scrutiny and under stress, and as an expression of radical order.

We devote ourselves first to the latter of the two.

Radical order is not available for comparison, neither to disorder nor to order of any other species. It carries within it a direct link to universal order, order per se, which allows us to make use of it as a sub-stratum. But here we run into the difficulty of verification, because we will wish to confirm, every step of the way, how this link is fashioned and upon what it relies for strength. The wish is understandable but must be ignored. The charge of pursuing phantasma may be borne in manly fashion. As long as we leave to chance what arises from chance and while we cleave to the simple repetition of time, as rhythm, as metre, as beat, as the unnumbered one-after-another occurrence of whatever occurs, we cannot go wrong, and we build us a foundation where previously nothing stood.

Every expression of radical order causes an impulse of finite reality to become a stimulus of infinite reality. The fact of the change delivers into our grasp the very shape of incidental physiognomy. Perhaps we take advantage of this right away for the purpose of other expressions of the same kind. Or we continue, as far as we may, experimentally or otherwise, with the deployment of fictive genera, to be exploited at another time. By fictive genera we mean all those corrective and proprietary cases of organic vitality through whose instrumentality we settle ourselves and permanently ease our states of life into eternal growth. Organic vitality in these cases is never topped by an aboriginal legitimacy or supported, openly or in secret, by the flesh of the tribe.

It is the flesh of the tribe that blocks all states in their formalized trends and that frustrates even significant solutions to the oldest problem imaginable: our sensation of one another. Why this constitutes a problem has long been forgotten and we only rack our brains from time to time in order to lock the door even more tightly against the commonweal. The flesh of the tribe is opposed manifestly to the flesh of Christ, and each of these excludes the other. The propaganda of popular governments would always divide this equation and assimilate where total enmity must reign.

We sense one another only while the fruits of our existence may continue to ripen; while our humanity may subsist in mutual consequence; upon the radical deportment of all old and unexemplary speciality in our doing and leaving in favour of a pronounced, profound perfection.

An element series as a phenomenon begins where our recognition of time has left off. Naturally the stress factor would pertain as readily to our vision of time as to our acceptance and abandonment of that which takes time, and so we agree to limit our progress to one side or the other of the equation while our eyesight holds out and our lucidity lasts. The scrutiny of felt data is initially moved by our best intentions in the direction of unavoidable collisions with late phenomena, with repressions of suitable experience, rejected merely on account of an inept faculty here or an inexact reading of circumstances there. The best precepts can only be followed while the pure heart is willing.

Do we not comprehend, then, why so many of our last works fail? We have severed the connection that bound us to one another by preferring a doubtful freedom on the basis of individual restraint. Only our total, and totally intelligent, abandonment to the course of goodness in our flesh as sons and daughters of god can help us where we need the help, the help none of us are able to define or to prescribe. Therefore it is incumbent upon our judgment to furnish us with the familial benefits of a unique education from the claimed loneliness of man, practically of man, woman and child.

*

The elements of our organic being must be maintained in states of control until such a time as our personality has become responsible. While the organism persists on the basis of an individual liberty we cannot really speak of elements as such, since a composition pertains, an aggregate of extreme modes materially subjected to forces that must remain indiscriminate and strange.

But individual liberty breaks down and an elementary product becomes available, first within reach of casual thought and later, when some experimentation has taken place, on the basis of reasonable thought.

We must look carefully now at the various effects produced when various qualities of thought, right to the point of pure and quantitative thought, extract elements, for the purpose of integration into one set or another of circumstances manufactured by that same thought. These effects are not always readily discernible because our thought tends to re-appropriate its first products. At the same time it serves our purpose to distinguish these initial lines of progress so as to be able to develop them as cleanly and as neatly as possible, so that they may eventually reside as perfect habits.

The most salutary approach, perhaps, succeeds in terms of local, physical inputs of energy, as yet dimly recognized, in the half-light of an old mood or through faulty faculties well intentioned. The probability, first of all, of such a field of experience, and the promise it seems to extend as a thing prone to mastery, may fail to appeal to us in its totality, but the appeal is there nevertheless, encouraging us to focus our attention invisibly for once, not on objects within or without. This invisibility of course holds the key and makes all the difference between a brutal attack on raw materials once again and the first beginnings of technical skill. Talent, or talents, are of no account here. Indeed, they often stand in the way, offering facility where eventually true ease will be required; also contracting the imagination, grossly at times, where eventually business may not rely on contracts.

Since objects are divisible to the point of invisibility, we need not concern ourselves with their presence as such. An initial energy input will meet with objection however and this must be countered with a degree of *a priori* knowledge. But this knowledge is never hard to get, since our input of energy, forceful or otherwise, had to rely on it as its source in the first place. So we find the knowledge to fit an objection to our act within the operational stimulus to that act in its very beginning, where it must be at least recorded. As the objection is overcome by dint of this knowledge, the element is withdrawn.

At this point an effect has not yet become accessible and one is faced with a potentially dangerous situation insofar as an elemental occurrence may attach indiscriminately and lead to waste and ruin. Attachment of any sort should therefore be strictly limited, disciplined in favour of contact and towards a reasonable end in time. Prior to any and all elemental occurrences, however, one may feel oneself forward, careful not to precipitate undue reaction, and in terms of felt being, or more accurately with the greatest possible respect to it, elements are connaturally invested as elementary substance. This is how it was in the beginning and one should not be too surprised that it should once again be this way.

Elementary substance is motivation as such. It is well worth our while that this should be thoroughly understood. Let us for a moment reflect on this shape. Motivation in truth needs no extraneous entity or body upon which to act. It is self-sustaining. It moves without being moved and it moves without necessarily setting anything in motion.

Only with a view to intuitive contemplation does elementary substance become productive. Indeed we may say that happy vision and intuitive contemplation together are the be-all and end-all where elementary substance in production is concerned. Out of production, or not yet in production, elementary substance has no particular existence and we say that it waits, or that it subsists. In subsistence it requires historical upkeep. This means that periodically an awareness of it is entertained. Elementary studies promote such awareness. It remains to be emphasized that elementary substance does not depend upon our awareness of it in order to continue to subsist and that our studies proceed when the proceed. Causality, morality and ethics cannot be involved with this. Elementary substance in subsistence and elementary studies complement each other, whenever and however they do.

Elementary subsistence (elementary substance in subsistence) excludes nothing and it includes everything. Not that it is everything but that it includes it, and not every thing, which implies production, but everything.

Because it includes everything it cannot be apprehended or given another name. But we may refer to it, in terms of our experience, as we wish. Still it subsists, unproduced and unproducing, not inert but early, trembling in readiness, and one may spin a cocoon of metaphor around it without harming it one whit; indeed, such a shell of elementary figures, made up of figurative substance, may stand for it and serve as introductory material, while any reflection on such a shell may produce a work of art.

Works or art, therefore, can be seen as products of a particular or specific reflection, not on particular or specific things, objects, bodies, entities, etc., but on figurative substance as a whole, or on the face of god.

But the face of god is wholly representative of himself, and it is this representation which has made credible our personal use of elementary substance and which has revealed to us, and for us, often through our trial and error, the image of our human perfection.

We may recall the dark days, when no perfect work suited us, and we strove to reject, from the image our faulty nature had produced, the fault that needfully persisted in it, while unknown to all but a few of us (and these few perceived it in an awful and transitory manner) it was the effort itself that did us good, not the end of our striving. Only a few, therefore, understood perfectly, and accepted wholeheartedly, how god's justice was not impugned by his choice of a few nor his mercy diminished by his election of some, but rather how this justice and mercy could not be installed by him in any other way, since thus it was good.

But elementary substance goes into production with the advent of love.

There is love as a power, which distinguishes between male and female.

There is love which reproduces. It separates the sexes.

There is love which draws us towards a common good. It does not distinguish but it is distinguished.

There is love which teaches and enlightens, and it adheres to all things.

These four are ordinary, and it is ordinary love that tests.

Then there is love that overcomes. Its strength lies in its overabundance.

There is love that limits and inhibits, for a purpose and so as to bring something about

There is love that leads. It demonstrates authority.

And finally there is love that rests in itself and seeks no end outside of itself.

Theses four are normal. The norm as such is wisdom, and it precedes or succeeds no other human function, which is why we call it the function. The norm, therefore is that wisdom which is the function.

Normal love and ordinary love together make up the eightfold pattern of love viewed as the product of elementary substance.

\*

We apply ourselves now to the first of these, which is love as a power.

In its first instance it rules and regulates material and governs the use of it. Our objective is to discover and to find out to what extent such material in use may be allowed to become organic and from what kind of a beginning it may take its lead, without succumbing to so many alterations to its supposed structure that it becomes unrecognizable.

Material in use becomes organic insofar as our appreciation of it is clean and quiet. We know that it has become organic and that it is so as soon as we feel free to share it freely with others. This feeling, then, is the test, in this case, of organic material.

Love as a power exists in its own right therefore as soon as the material it rules and regulates and the use of which it governs has become organic, which we know when we feel free to share it with others, and to share it freely. Organic material, therefore, is common property; while it belongs to all of us and to each one of us it cannot belong to one of us or to some of us exclusively.

Prior to its existence in its own right, love as a power has potential value, and this is where the measured character of its material organization is of the essence. In our philosophy we have dealt severally with measurement as an intrinsic factor. Here we come to it in full appreciation once again of the difference it makes and mindful of our cognizance of it.

Material in use may be allowed to become organic to the extent of our fullest appreciation of it as measured quality. Once we disregard, or even ignore this measured quality, we must assume that measurement is needfully up to us and then we strive to control and to get under our control, and this must always seem to succeed to a degree and it must always fail in fact to a degree. There is no real satisfaction in it.

We may learn to recognize that we are on the track leading nowhere as soon as we want to bring material in use under our control, and the thing to do then is simply to leave off. There is no alternative. Attempts to justify and to rationalize are wastes of time and effort.

We know that we are on the right track however while our appreciation of material in use is clean and quiet. To persevere in this direction means to accumulate organic material. Here perseverance is of the essence. Without it we indulge, like hypocrites, in self-congratulation; like dolts in complacency.

Simply to persevere for the love of it is unsurpassable, and next to it comes our perseverance for an eternal beginning, which is the same, though eventually. Such a beginning subordinates time past, present and future to the eternal moment, without subjecting anything temporary or contemporary to our intellect or will. We call it an eternal beginning because material in use is rendered organic insofar as an introduction to it of sensed phenomena establishes an exact replica in the world. This exact replica is always of the world. That it is established in the world makes it a beginning and that it is exact makes it eternal.

Material in use has no structure and it is without a structure. This seems to be a terribly difficult lesson to learn for all of us, and those who by now still are not sure what we mean by material in use are probably looking for something, for something structured. For it was always the structure of things that recommended them to our individuality, since our individuality sought to enhance itself, to confirm itself, to find itself in its own likeness. But our mirror image cannot save us from ourselves. Those who sense this often try to go against their worst impulses by altering the structure of things against the inclination of their individuality, or else they destroy things in the hope that this will have the effect which cannot be achieved except that they give up their individuality. While it distinguishes them from the dead, whose individuality is the structure of things, it does not distinguish them in their own right, for we are not distinguished until our individuality is gone and the truth grows where individuality had usurped its place.

Once material in use has become organic, we refer to it as weakness and as infirmity.

By weakness we mean that particular quality of mind and body that locates for us and for our faculties an indispensible root of reality. Where our weakness resides, there are we captivated by a radical exception to the rule of our humanity, and this makes the weakness an indicator of real growth. The rule of our humanity usually implies a settled activity within a coercive frame of reference. Weaknesses unsettle us and disturb conditions for us, not indiscriminately, but in such a way that we may, if we wish, disentangle ourselves from wrong commitments, and often it takes just such an unsettling influence to render us more susceptible to the increased investment of our inheritance.

Now the difference between weakness and infirmity is one of gender. We are made aware of this even as we disengage our vision from the numerous claims made on it by properties other than those of the light, and little by little our moods fade, our sensations become explicit and we perceive the inner workings of our organism; of that, in short, which contains our inclinations and leanings, our tendencies and likenesses, our proclivities and taste preferences. The difference in gender lets us see in fact how weaknesses and infirmities in particular can accumulate for no other reason than to help us become aware of our various organic intensities. These are not as simple and as clear cut as one might suppose after centuries of natural-supernatural pictography in this light. An organic intensity contains implicit functions of its own, and yet, taken on its own and scrutinized against a background of abstracted material, organic intensity as such lacks all those virtual characteristics that would allow us to credit its sheer importance. This is because organic intensity as such can only be viewed out of practice, in reflection upon itself as it were, and therefore as a theoretic construct, laudable in its own right, as an achievement of the human intellect for the purpose of self-knowledge, and even useful at times as a sort of concept ladder, or as a back-and-forth of emotion values, interesting and sometimes entertaining, but from our present point of view inherently lame.

What interests us much more, especially as we have love as a power at heart, is the organic intensity in the concrete, and, more to the point, this one right here. It separates the down-to-earth spirits from those that prefer to remain air-borne for reasons best not discussed here. It links up our lesser with our greater values in the name not of good talking or even good doing, but of good living.

Let us take this organic intensity right here and call it sorrow. All that it means comes from what it means to us just now, and yet we make no attempt to divorce its impression or impact from the general or traditional one. Neither do we ask sorrow for what, or from what source? No object or subject has a claim on it, since our personal claim on it maintains itself.

This sorrow, then, activates in us both momentary illusions, which we ignore, and substantial features of reality, to which we devote ourselves.

This devotion is essentially little. There is nothing demonstrative about it or in any way self-assertive. It is not a dignified devotion, nor does it stand on ceremony. It may arise as certainly from a memory or our childhood as it must be effaced by prestige and self-esteem.

This little devotion is extremely effective when applied voluntarily, especially prior to any constraint to do so, to the sorrow at hand for example. Not that we expect any sensations of success or failure. Not that we would compare our state of being to superior powers or to great principalities. Far be it from us to look back on any comparative states. The very mildness of our temperament might serve us as the best test for the correctness of our endeavour. And of course there is the blank certainty of mind. Not that our mind is blank, but its certainty remains so. We look forward to nothing and to everything.

The sorrow we mean materially enhances our outlook on life for it lets us care where previously we could not care. Like all good beginnings, this one too is small, so small you would hardly notice it. We are given an element of courage to care. As a direct result of this we are proportionately trusted, and even though such trust may initially catch us off guard, we find it eventually in ourselves to respond and to trust in turn. The intensity of our organism makes itself felt throughout all this, by no means as a romantic strain but as an operational trend, to which we cannot help but assent, neither could we dissent, since consciousness of the feeling accompanies the freedom to choose wisely, while no one would wish to choose unwisely.

The operational trend of our organic intensity is sexual in character, and so in this case, being male, I care particularly for all those aspects of creation that are mistakenly supposed to be unredeemed. Neglect and unjustified ignorance look to me for correction and trust forces me to act where I see no previous reason to act. The force involved is infallible. Its cause resides in the organic intensity itself and we choose wisely not to question its outcome. A free man can neither want nor have the right to go against his freedom. With respect to one another we say that this force is safe.

Love as a power automatically issues in safe force. We need no sacramental benediction to prepare us for this force nor to remind us of it, since it is rooted wholly in reality, which makes it holy in nature. Neither, of course, can this force be abused, since it cannot even be applied. It cannot be made to operate, nor can it be allowed or encouraged to operate, nor can conditions be made favourable for it. The safe force that issues from love as a power is in itself terminally designed, personally suitable, generally unavailable, justly merciful.

*

Love which reproduces can be followed up intellectually, but only while the flesh, or the totality of felt phenomena, has the capacity to stimulate our understanding. This is why we say that love which reproduces separates the sexes, because due to our understanding of all phenomena we recognize the imprint of sex on all that is either male or female. The original distinction of male and female, wherever it occurs, is not a separation, to put it bluntly, and so that reproduction may occur there must be a separation, at one level or another, between female and male. This separation is always accompanied by a degree of anxiety and it is the personal examination of this anxiety, the acceptance of responsibility for it, that allows reproduction to become human.

The personal examination of sexual anxiety creates, initially, a backlog of loose imagination and a disparity of concerned thought. Feeling, for a while, is turned inside out, due to the removal of a unified object or a whole subject. One might say that feeling is encouraged to turn towards itself, so running the risk of turning against itself. The object of this particular exercise is that feeling may become clean. Only clean feeling, insofar as it stems from the caring heart, may eventually support and sustain reproduction in its entirety. Take such feeling away from reproduction and the latter is left desolate and unpronounced. The pronounced aspect of reproduction ends in the product as a being in itself, while desolate reproduction leaves the product bereft.

Feeling that turns against itself is left isolate, or in isolation. Isolate feeling is a morbid state and can only be expurgated, from without. So we need a companion to rid us of this. We should not expect such an expurgation to feel pleasant, since morbid feelings have adopted a false pleasure and they always manage to insist. One can recognize morbid feelings by their insistence on themselves, even in the face of goodness, and hence what is required may amount to shock. But this can be discussed when we come to love that overcomes.

Clean feeling requires that the imagination become at least serviceable, rather than clinging to whatever object or whatever subject just then presents itself. Our imagination learns to be of service as soon as it recognizes itself in creations around it. Now there is no more reason to stray because all the alternatives are equally endowed with reason, while it takes the particular and persistent commitment to the one to bring that reason to the fore.

Unique reason, brought to the fore by the particular and persistent commitment of serviceable imagination, states itself viably in terms of straight thought. The disparity of concerned thought due to our examination of sexual anxiety pervades until such a time as is ushered in by our willingness to persevere in this examination to the point of a rational idea, which we may hold for a time.

Love reproduces again and pushes on, investing clean feeling wholly in behaviour, or in holy behaviour. How we do what we do has now become a matter of distinction, irrespective of how it looks, to others or to ourself.

This peculiar investment of clean feeling in holy behaviour extinguishes automatically all thought that is less than subtle and other than meek.

The distinct imagination, in turn, is given an illuminatory frame of reference, so that it impinges upon the light and the light on it. So we say that the imagination glows. But it does so periodically.

Rational ideas meanwhile take their course, whether we hold them or not. Most rational ideas nourish the mind unwittingly and they develop in secret. This notion, that rational ideas must be held and fostered in order to make a difference, is quite wrong. It suffices that the idea has once had an effect on us as such. It is very possible, and even likely, that we continue to act in some way according to that idea unwittingly. This is the case whether the idea is good or bad. The only intelligent response to this insight is that we set out to realize our ideas, good or bad, and during the process of realization we winnow the grain from the chaff. Obviously a bad idea cannot be intelligently realized, since the growing intelligence insists on conscientious confirmation. But bad ideas can become modes of abuse even before we become conscious of our participation in such abuse, so that the intelligent realization of ideas becomes worthwhile even on the basis of precaution. Bad ideas in this way are extirpated.

A rational idea intelligently realized gives rise, at first in fluctuation and then steadily, to finished reproductions and perfect works. We need make no allowance here for a difference between the two. Our concern is for love that reproduces to easily find its predestined end, which is eternal life in status.

It should be added here that the separate sexes attract or repel each other and that this must be taken into account when we distinguish between male and female. The attractive aspect of sex may well negate the love that instigated the separation of the sexes in the first place, just as the repulsion may augment that same love, depending again on the intelligence at work. A lack of intelligence renders the separate sexes destructive from the start. An optimum of intelligence on the other hand renders the separate sexes supremely creative and they join as one, leaving nothing of a difference between them to the imagination.

The imprint of sex, by the way, is never merely the cause of propagation. What we unduly question at times when this imprint of sex, often forcibly, sometimes violently, comes to our attention and disturbs for us the status quo of a mental picture of ourselves, has to do with the popular features of sex as annexed by the popular mentality and as collective opinion would have it. The gain that is ours due to this imprint of sex on our various faculties, due, in other words, to the capacity of our faculties to undergo a separation from such faculties of an opposite sex, and finally of course due to the opposite nature of sex as such, varies with time, but never with respect to its absolute coherence as cosmic substance in time present, future and past. The ability to view time present, future and past as one depends entirely on such cosmic substance, and it is a view held by those who may well be called the internal guardians of eternal life, for without them the human species would long ago have perished, to be swallowed by the populace of this earth.

And again, we can keep up appearances with respect to our sexual capacity for a while, but then atrophy sets in, as in the case of that cursed fig tree, since no use of these faculties means abuse of their powers.

The imprint of sex, where it is given, may lead to doubt and duplicity as readily as to our special recognition as members of the human family. Whether one or the other, this is the challenge we face as potential representatives of mankind.

What we call mankind is in fact the inherited aspect of sexual difference. Mankind is engendered. The imprint of sex alleviates the need for mankind to be constantly regenerated. This constant regeneration was of critical importance while the final character of mankind was still in doubt, and it paid each and every one of us to reckon with expulsion from mankind as a possible occurrence. This also meant that we held on tight to what we possessed, and rightly so, for our inheritance was yet in transit. We possessed the species of mankind, and we knew that for mankind to come to fruition this species needed to be transferred in tact, to the hearts and minds of men, there to be invested.

The imprint of sex may therefore be viewed also as an historical occurrence. Various complexes of popular opinion and taste bear testimony to that. At the same time we should harbour no illusions as to the critical decisiveness of this imprint. It parted the spirits. Some took stock of themselves and gave in

36

to the change in the name of someone greater, for it is true greatness that was at stake here. Others fought the change, for the sake of continued lawfulness, and they were broken by it. But the great majority of course noticed nothing, nothing except the removal of inhibitions and the dissipation of constraints. As a consequence the majority, this generation, was dissipated and removed.

The division of the flesh therefore carries this imprint of sex. Where the flesh is divided it attracts our influence so that we who are one flesh may express our being there. We exert our influence where the flesh is divided, and we do this as an act of the love that reproduces. Now we may well understand how this works. To arrest the divided flesh in repose we instil an image of this imprint of sex and it takes hold there, until such a time as may suffice to act out this image historically, which happens, of course, with respect to one or more than one of us. What we cannot do is follow up the progress of such an image in action since it must obey the lead of its own specific properties to the point of the emergency, or *an* emergency. What emerges is as yet unknown. Then circumstances are creatively altered to accommodate the emergency.

One can see how the flesh makes for the figure of this process. We, in turn, apprehend this figure and it leads us to the process. To be caught up in the process, with no recourse to the figure, adds an element of sacrifice which is of not much use. The immersion in the figure, to the detriment of intelligence, can be avoided.

All in all we have before us here a complete picture of the sexual aspect of creation, a workable facsimile and its counterpart in logic; in short, what would be required if one chose such a path to life in greater abundance.

Human reproduction is impossible without love. Humanity is the essence of being and love is its gift to creation. Whatever truly is, is human, and its reproduction through love creates more love. God is, and so he is human, and we know him as Jesus Christ, the cornerstone in the edifice of creation. But Jesus Christ lives in the spirit, which is to say in reality, and so he takes us to our father, where we live with him in light and joy and gladness. This is what it means then, to really live, to live in reality, with our father and his son Jesus Christ, and in the company of our mother Mary, who assumes the love of her son Jesus Christ and calls us, her sons and daughters, to the love in which we may triumph.

*

We go on now to the love which draws us towards a common good. It is distinguished and can therefore be held in esteem.

The common good we mean is the kingdom, or the kingdom of heaven on earth. By earth we do not mean this earth. We might also call the kingdom the world without end, or the world, which is not this world, for this world has come to its end.

Fist of all we are drawn by this love to the centre of the universe, which is the earth. We do not mean the middle of the universe, but its centre. When people regard the universe as though it were all space, with things or objects or bodies in it, then they soon look for a middle to this space, and of course since they mean all space they can only go on to say what definitely is not and cannot be the middle, such as the earth, and they are, as usual, quite right in their way, not because they tell us anything about the earth or about the universe, but simply because according to a wrong description the appearance of something cannot be as it is described. But enough of this. The universe and the earth have as much to do with time as with space, and as much again with the elements, so that we may state without fear of contradiction that the earth, in reality, is the centre of the universe.

Now to be drawn implies motion, and when we get to where we are drawn we are in perfect motion, which is rest. But to be at rest at the centre of the universe, which is to say on the earth, means to be at home on the earth, and surely this is what we all want. It only depends on what we mean by home, by earth, by want, etc; which is not an entirely facetious comment these days, when arbitrary opinion seems to hold sway.

For the kingdom, or the world (not this world) to be rightly seen and understood as a common good we must share it with one another as a family, and of course we cannot do otherwise, since this family has the father as its father, the mother as its mother, the son as its brother and reality as its being.

In reality we are drawn to the earth, then, as the seat of our family. Here our family is situated and we need look no further. When we do look further afield we fail to come to terms withal those terrestrial forces by which we then suppose our nature to be ruled. We end up by dividing everything into nature and supernature, to the detriment of our everyday experience. It helps to remember that all that was made in the beginning was redeemed in the end. From such a memory stems the very acute conviction that the love which draws us towards a common good may indeed be trusted, that we can relax into it, that the tendency we feel often requires only the screening by our awareness and it transports us safely.

That this love draws us can only be experienced; but what an experience! It makes sense primarily as the fullness and ripeness of time. Not that we see or hear first, but it affects us how we are, and how we hear and see. We understand also why so much could not be said until now, because it dictates its own terms and the expression of everything else in those terms afterwards. If we believe that we have narrowly escaped the confines of false instruction, or that we might have settled in a lesser evil rather than striving towards a greater good, there is no need to go back on this. It may have been so. On the other hand there is no need to plan out our future meticulously in accordance with the past. There is no real future in that, but only a poor copy of the past plus the danger of catastrophe. If we lack the courage to become responsible citizens, our courage may be required elsewhere, towards another end.

The popular notion of love that draws flees for appearances into illusion. But illusion holds no water and supports no weight, so that the return to appearances becomes inevitable, followed by the incarceration of the heart; and the mind does the incarcerating, that is what hurts most. One sees that one damns oneself and cannot hinder it.

As an idea, what we can expect at the centre of the universe is the impulsion to create, and this idea, when realized, means creativity as such. Now we must define this creativity as the exercise of Christ. For just as god is not separate from his creation or from his creatures, so as to be all the more distinct, so does Christ move with us and in us, and we move with him and in him. Christ's exercise is the joyful activity of our life. Through creativity, and as creative beings, we fully live on the earth. But creativity is the exercise of Christ. Our creativity does not end in things or objects, in bodies or subjects, but Christ is its end. This is extremely important, for in our extremity we become prone to making the mistake that this exercise is an end in itself. At the same time it cannot be stated too clearly that creativity leaves a record. This record attests more or less succinctly to the glory and majesty of Christ. Now since Christ comes in glory to the detriment of all those who hate him, this record of our creativity retains an element of choice, and since Christ comes in majesty to the chagrin of those who have despaired of him, this record of our creativity retains an element of chance. These two elements, of choice and of chance, allow those to participate who would falsify the record and they are freed of their falsehood or denied it. Therefore let the record show by these elements how we fare.

The coming of Christ in glory and majesty fills us with such a joy that we forget who we are and where we are in comparison to others. But our creativity meets up with that which goes against Christ and it draws the strength from it. The love which draws us towards a common good is fortified in turn by creative doing. Anti-creative effects are not so much overcome, therefore, as absorbed and assimilated.

And here we touch on the special instrumentality of Christ's church. It thrives on opposition in this peculiar way.

All the effects of Christ's church are especially and specifically creative, and the sum-total of all of these effects is in fact Christ's church. We can see that this has nothing to do with creativity as it appeals to the popular imagination. Popularity may in fact be described as the characteristic expression, or picture, of the demonic. And the demonic opposes creativity at large. But though our creativity is strengthened as it meets up with the demonic, we cannot choose or elect to meet up with the demonic, nor can we intend to draw strength from it. While we could, and if we did so, we sowed the wind and reaped the whirlwind.

For the sake of precision we add here that while not all creative effects are especial and specific, those that are not are not yet so, and they cannot be otherwise lauded. Perhaps they remind us of a critical remnant in ourselves.

But we freely praise the distinguished love, and the creativity that is one with it, while the record is beyond, or outside of judgment.

In our own estimation this love may be freely indulged in, while in the estimation of others it simply does not exist, so no problem needs to be solved on that score. While we let the record speak for itself, others may tend to separate words out of it, to divorce the letter from the meaning. They cannot help themselves and we cannot even attempt to help them.

It nearly always surprises us, though, when we fail in this. The mood of the moment cheats us of the appropriate insight and we end up caring in a direction whence no good can come to us. We try to alter the state of our affairs and make ourselves unpopular. Then, on reflection, we try a more genuine tack and chalk up the episode to experience.

*

This brings us to the love that teaches and enlightens.

There is nothing so splendid as the promises kept by the life that is eternal, and this thought brings to mind our own being prior to the advent of time, to the event of the logos. No man can remember more than he is worth, but he should remember all of it, and to this end he is under obligation. He feels that he ought to enlist all of his mental energies in the search for the cause of that obligation. He must stand firm, in the face of all rational and collective opinion to the contrary, on his basic objection to a calculated, premeditated point of view when it comes to an explanation of his origin.

As far as our gaze can reach, unless we get sidetracked by the adventitious maze of appearances, a settled terrain of real being invites us to inquire and to explore. Being reasonable at heart, we wonder why we might inquire and to what end we might explore, and even from the standpoint of ready experience we notice how this 'might' seems somehow able and willing to balance the 'ought' of that other urgency. The promise of a final good plays into this of course, but more immediately we feel the satisfaction of contradictories resolved, of a struggle alleviated, of a pressure removed. Those few happy souls who decide early on that 'in their beginning lies their end' and to whom this is more than a mildly poetic formula, are to be envied, I suppose. But better than envy is imitation. And so we could do worse than to listen to what they have to say, especially if at first it strikes us as an awkward and uncomfortable message.

What our conscience tells us we should, and what our senses tell us we want, are really and truly in the end one and the same. Remove one of these and the other becomes effete and a caricature. Assume they arise from a single will and at once there is peace. So easy, and yet so rare. Around every corner the children of hate suspect a triumph or a defeat. They cannot agree within themselves and so they must disagree with each other. The alert eye recognises at once that the disparity sets in and the mind heals it, since that is its nature, unless that nature has become perverse in the service of itself.

Man's search for his origin encompasses his existence like a protective skin and unless he searches diligently and wisely that skin breaks. Then follows the mad capering of the disowned animal. The conclusion to every undertaking is momentary. Trials are left unattended and lead to no new growth. One rules out even the possibility of success of any but the most confectionary endeavours and these are then glorified out of all proportion until judgment itself it lost.

When love teaches, it takes advantage of native wisdom and this is a gift. The human being at birth is endowed with such wisdom and it keeps him in contact with his inheritance as a representative of mankind. In the vast majority of cases this native wisdom is soon lost and an inert intelligence takes its place.

But where love teaches, native wisdom quickly develops and the human being emerges, eager to experience life.

This is where love enlightens. It begins by pointing out the unique difference between living and merely existing. It goes on to show the three-dimensionality of living, in terms of the truth, the light and the way, in comparison to the one- or two-dimensional existence of the so-called human animal, as it rejects life and as it insists on this rejection, which it calls individuality.

After an appropriate time the comparison is dropped because it is realized that mere existence has passed away and that life is eternal. But eternal life encompasses all things even as love adheres to them. We do not love these things, therefore, but love adheres to them, and so we continue to learn and to grow in wisdom.

The adherence of love to things renders them mobile so that they become susceptible to our influence. Immobile things are inherently repulsive and their proximity misleads. The mobility itself of things has a significance for us, or we might say that it carries and transmits a burden of proof. But this burden is light. It comes as a surprise to those who search for significance behind the surface of things that the mobility itself of these things has our interest at heart. There is no need first to strip off a common body in order to reveal a secret ghost. Mobility is not a phenomenon left over upon degrees of abstraction either. It links into our own sense apparatus and an excitement results, an excitation of sense material and a stimulation of sensible matter.

The mobility of things to which love adheres excites in us various states of perfection, and these would be mobilized, so here we have warranted practical motivations towards as yet unknown perfect ends. As long as we do these things we cannot fail. We will not be able to do them except perfectly, so we give our all and we proceed uncritically. Of course we can take no pride in such deeds – which is another point in their favour.

Whatever offends us may be referred to such status of perfection. The offensive thing is understood as an unwilling carrier of a burden, and this gives us an opportunity to do what we can only do perfectly. If a classified thing were to offend, it would refer itself to a state of perfection and an emotion would let us concentrate our faculties. The emotion would have that purpose and that purpose alone. We would not be able to apply it otherwise or to ascertain it in any way in itself.

The sum total of our emotion at a given moment in time may be practically compressed and made to serve in the interest of a perfect deed. This compression becomes emphatic for no other reason than to exert on our physical environment an exceeding force, and to do this until that force is recognized.

An exceeding force probes environmental conditions and limitations to the end of an accumulating sensation. There are no external facets to such a sensation and if we were to look for them we should feel disappointment. Also we should ask ourselves periodically how such a sensation might be attained, as a type on call, or analogically, because without making a habit of it we still may instigate action from it, or from the sensation's effect, reflectively, depending on our make-up. But the action which stems from such sensation always had communal purport: it may seem senseless to me at the moment, as the instigator, but I proceed nevertheless in the fullest awareness of this communal and peripheral engagement of present results. To insist on a special comprehension would curtail the supply of sensible and factual stuff and the process would come to a halt.

Organic sensation is what we call the activity of our senses when under the ordinance of an environment that is being probed by an exceeding force.

The environment, we must imagine, has in such a case impressed upon it from within, not from without, an affliction of ours, passionately felt, and since this affliction goes to the very root of our being, which is to say of our human being, it cannot help but be shared in some fashion by that which is environmental to us.

We could proceed from the opposite direction and mention environment inflicting upon us a less than human condition to which we may respond in a forceful way, but one thing at a time.

That the cosmos participates, in some manner of form, in each and every human predicament may be understood, therefore, and goes hand in hand with our view of man as both the crown of creation and the instrument of perdition, and so whether we deal with man as a purpose or as a hazard, the link itself holds. Human being cannot be taken separately from all other being. However the particular advantage we take of this link, in love, to espouse the elementary being of things, even of things that are in themselves elementary, necessities a collective concentration of all of our emotional impulses and moments, (momenta), in the enlistment towards an energetic and energized wholeness in our organic reality. The ordinance of our afflicted environment appeals to us in terms of work and we find that in our work is made manifest to us our actual oneness with everything and our deeply rooted responsibility for everything else. Hence the express notion of authority from without and consequently, not subsequently or prior, the concept of authority from within. The experience and investment of this authority shows how both are one, so that our taste for the notion and our use of the concept are correctly understood as additional benefits to, not as deficiencies of, the organic wholeness, in love that teaches and enlightens, of our competent authority.

Competent authority is sufficiently genuine and authentically fit. It reaches easily beyond ideas and principles to a particular moment of life. Here it allows us to act in full possession of our memory and perfectly at ease with respect to the effect of our action. There is no need, therefore, to employ deceitful means in order to avoid a confrontation with foolishness. Neither does competent authority ever meet with rebellion. It rests totally within itself with respect to its effectiveness. Whatever trials it comes across tend automatically to uplift it to greater intensity. Except for moments of inner renewal, competent authority remains constant except for its intensity, which fluctuates with the requirement for it. A check on this intensity and a steadying influence on its fluctuation is our temperament insofar as it has become mild.

Mild temperament together with competent authority lead to wise action.

*

Ordinary love tests, we have said, and therefore pain is never far removed from it. Now without wishing to mystify the feeling and the experience of pain we would like to have a closer look at it so as to become more familiar with it as an element of

46

love, and of ordinary love. We take care not to widen our sphere of interest beyond whatever associations with pain that can be made in the state of consciousness, for here we actually deal with pain on its own ground, not as a cause or an effect of imagined or pictured categories.

No one can be expected to like pain; that would be absurd. But there is nothing that says we are not allowed to view it experimentally.

This implies a high degree of intellectual stamina. Only time will tell how we have succeeded, but succeed we must.

Ordinary love, as we have described and shown it above, always makes a specific appeal to our willingness not so much to suffer but to suffer for someone. It will always matter to us, of course, who this someone is, and we cannot go wrong if we begin with the one person who always had our wellbeing at heart, and who profits from it if we suffer for him insofar as it brings us all closer together. But insofar as we suffer for one another we also suffer for him, so it comes to the same.

The nature of our suffering, then, is dictated by who he is for whom we suffer, and who he is brings us face to face with what he has done. When we bring to mind then that he suffered for us to the point of dying for us and that in drawing us to him now he is willing for us to have that in mind, we need no further conclusion to be drawn before we define suffering as the knowledge of pain in his name. The pain will stop when it stops and it should not be our primary concern to make the pain stop, but it should be our secondary concern, a concern born from the willingness to suffer.

And when pain has robbed us of the ability to think properly, we must trust that our circumstances will somehow supply us with a cure, since he who has died for us is in us even as we are in him. In other words, while he is within us we also know that he is around.

The sensation of pain in this frame of reference becomes a vicarious thing, which is very important, for while we sense this pain we feel compassion for, are compassionately inclined towards, one who sensed this pain in itself. And there is no question that it was the very same pain. Sensation inheres. It leaves no trace and yet we may assume a carrier for it through time. How this comes to be is a matter for those who must touch before they feel, and they are given their own way of finding out.

The birth of compassion from pain, therefore, is not extraordinary, but quite ordinary. His passion begets our compassion by way of the pain we suffer. How this happens can only be described in terms of preventative measures against painless states where suffering is rejected for no good reason. Isolated states of feeling are always suspect and to be avoided, especially if we can tell that we fear to be without them. No separation should be allowed to creep between what we do feel and what we wish to feel. We may feel poorly and we may wish to feel good, not an uncommon wish, but it is no use wishing to feel good unless we know what we mean by that and unless we refrain from clinging to some imagined or recalled likeness of good feeling. There is no progress from one feeling to the next, except through thought. Feeling that clings to, or strives after, its own likeness regresses. Now when we suffer pain we may strive to accumulate a degree of pain or we may let ourselves be quite assimilated by the pain, but mainly we extend ourselves in the direction of that pain as a vicarious thing, as something that comes to us once suffered through, as it were, and we may manage, by suffering it again, to unite ourselves more closely with him who suffered it initially. So no pain can come to us in a raw state, first of all, and whatever pain comes to us does so as an opportunity. It does not come as a personal invitation however, so we have no cause for a fanatical suffering. The opportunity is given and we choose to take it to the limits of our strength. And what we cannot suffer we endure.

By the same token can we see god from our pure heart as we wish, but god sees us as he sees fit, to help us become more worthy of him.

Time and again objections arise in us to what our feelings have learned long ago and we mistake the resulting sense of doubt for a realistic hindsight. Science helps us out of such tight spots by offering us the benefits of no uncertain knowledge without tying us to the defects of indiscriminate subject matter. We may once again be purified, with the additional assurance that we have gained somehow in the overall view of things, even though it may take a while before we can say exactly how we have gained.

Science tempts us only to become greater than ourselves; when we give in to the temptation we commit our faculties and energies to a course of action from which death itself cannot keep us. We lose our selves and find ourselves in science.

*

We go on now to discuss the love that overcomes.

It must find in us somewhere a longing to be united to god. Once this longing is established, we find ourselves beset, first, by doubts and miseries, and for a time we may well wish we had never been born, for while our longing dies like a seed we have nothing to keep us sane but the hope of renewed favour. Then when this love comes, it deceives our reaction to it by planting in us various hopes and happy anticipations, but these are only to keep us up to the mark, and while we are glad to grasp at them, we are even more glad to let them go when this love reveals itself finally within us.

The love that overcomes is not at our disposal. If we ever feel that we can manipulate its effects it soon reminds us of the various trials and errors that would be required if we had to rid ourselves of such a false notion.

But the tribal customs of people make this love difficult. They claim it for themselves in the name of group instinct and they pursue it on the basis of mass appeal, to sell their commodities and to appease their panic before the truth. So from early on we tend to despise it and to find its champions contemptible. As for the substitute we try to produce ourselves, it disappoints exceedingly because invariably our demands on it become excessive. If anyone asked us then which we preferred, to be loved or to be hated, we should probably choose the latter, because it reminds us less of our worthless selves. What we find most abhorrent, however, is not our inability to love entirely as we choose, but the apparent delight others take in our inability to cope. For the love that overcomes must first overcome us. Perhaps it would be smart to lend it a hand. The main difficulty lies in our unwillingness to be judged. Why this should trouble us can only be understood when we admit to a fault in us. How this fault came about is not important, but only that it exists and that it persists. Since god is perfect, a commitment to god seems to demand a similar perfection, and yet we have a fault, so we hide. Consequently only through Jesus, who has forgiven us our faults, can we approach god, so that the judgment rids us of the fault rather than getting rid of us as we fear. But then again we are ashamed, I suppose, to let someone do for us what it has always been our greatest source of self-esteem to insist on having done ourselves; to suggest that only Jesus has forgiven our sins initially outrages our sense of self-sufficiency, and only rarely does it come to the point where we forgive each other's faults in Jesus' name.

The most basic fault, therefore, is  not to accept Jesus. All other faults can be traced to it. The fact that Jesus can be so despicable only shows us what we are, for he is not so in truth but only in our imagination. We condemn him to death in ourselves and in each other because he reminds us of the true state of our affairs and hides nothing from us. If we wish to know him as he really is, we must allow him to return to us completely as a person, as someone with will and intellect, with plans of his own. Our father's kingdom on earth is not brought about in the privacy of our minds where we exclude Christ nor can it be watched at a distance from the newspapers

So if I am to be overcome, what can I do to expedite this process? Because I can well be aware of myself, more frequently in sorrow than in joy. But this does not constitute self-awareness. I am nothing by myself, separate from you and from god, and therefore I cannot experience any form of sorrow for myself in such a state. Whatever sorrow I feel must stem in some way from a connection or contact with god, even though it might only betoken the breaking of such a contact, which is rare; in any case, where life is, there is Jesus, and where Jesus is, there is our father.

My self insists on itself. My self is the one non-element with which I must reckon. How does it come into being? There it is! How does it manage to keep going? While I believe in it. There is nothing like faith in my self to propagate its existence. Remember that we are writing the science of the elements, and that we have arrived at the point of intersection where the various paths of the elements cross. To know of the possible existence of this non-element, which is my self, or your self, for that matter, is extremely important and we may develop a fine sensitivity to its presence wherever it occurs.

But first let us state once and for all time that your self and my self are one and the same. There is only one self. It will always insist that it is the greatest or the most, implying a multiplicity or at least a plurality, and this is the first trick it plays on us, pretending to be more than one. In this way it institutes a system of competition and we get involved in trying to top one another where we should strive to be at the bottom.

The duplicity of my self is its main weapon. If its duplicity is denied it, our self right away plunges us into the doldrums to prove to us that without it we can take no interest in anything. How does it hope to succeed in this, and why is this a very clever thing for it to do, from its point of view? Because we like to take an interest in things that grow, and because we seem prone to mistake material increase for growth. So what better way to reclaim an interest in life than to throw ourselves head first into some accumulation of matter? We should wait the paralysis out. The duplicity of our self knows no better field of activity, where it can keep dividing in two as it seems eternally to produce more, than our competitive notion of mere progress. Mere progress deceives, and nothing deceives like mere progress. Duplicity and deception are the two legs on which our self strides down the avenue, to the envy of passersby.

If growth interests you, wait for the one that comes without appointment. It begins imperceptibly. It starts so small that none will pick it out. It derives its sustenance from nothing perishable. Our life itself indicates its progress, nothing temporal outside of it.

Once its duplicity has been denied and its deception negated, our self plays its trump card and makes us fear for our life. It does this so well that multitudes pay with their soul for this fear. We tremble before the onslaught of real physical dangers. The security of the home, the bosom of the family, the comforts and excesses of the flesh, all these are threatened and faced with extinction. We end by defending our self. Fear withdraws the distinction.

Christ teaches us what to fear and what not to fear. The simple operation of our feeling on this point separates high status from hysteria, a contrary will from the fluctuations of morbidity.

So, to duplicity and deception this self of ours adds doubt, the doubt that makes us fear for our very existence, as if our father cared less for us than for stones, and this doubt should be ignored. What, such a childish remedy for the most sophisticated of all evils? Yes, precisely, though more childlike than childish.

Ignore the doubt inspired by your self even as a child ignores the face of a danger it has never seen. Sure, we can ignore what we wish. Our vanity alone counsels us to persuade our self to be a., realistic, b., consequent, c., truthful; but how can a non-element become an element? No argument can be devised so that foolishness will admit to its foolishness, or our self to its false essence. Avoid the contagion of dispute. Flee from the errors of a mind zealous in self-advertisement. Give wide berth to the magnificent heroes of independent character, to the superstars of individual flair, because in their hearts they harbour the grand doubt, which doubts everything but its self.

The love that overcomes must first overcomes us, we have said, and this is how we become separated from our self, so that I am able to love you especially and you are able to love me especially, which means that the love each one of us has for the other gains its essential character from our love of Christ, so that we are able to give what is unique, you what only you can give and I what only I can give. Only insofar as we love Christ, or one another as he loved us, are we truly ourselves. Only insofar as I know and believe that Christ loves me can I truly say: I am this, or: I do that.

But Jesus loves us today and rules us too, so that we cannot go against him and in his kingdom we can do no wrong. As his love overcomes us our self is cast off and our hearts are given the final laws of his kingdom. As this love overcomes whatever does not pertain to his kingdom we grow in stature and the kingdom on earth in us. For we live on the earth where we do god's will and Christ Jesus lives here with us, sharing with us his love for the Father and our Father's special love for him. This is the love that overcomes, so that impurities are removed and imperfections eradicated.

*

We come now to the love that limits and inhibits, for a purpose, and so as to bring something about.

Its mark is the root of charity, and we need to look at it in this light if we are not to be taken in by what pretends to be its opposite, an elucidation of mere mind.

The limit of love is always persuasive and never coercive. Any amount or degree of inhibition may be sustained by the body or mind while contention is stopped in its tracks. We may ask how far we may go before a limitation is imposed, or we may go as far as we can and then recognize the inhibition, the main point worthy of our attention being the total and utter absence of self-imposed limits or inhibitions. Where love does the work we ourselves step aside. We respond to the fact that we are always loved and we respond, or more accurately: correspond, to that love itself. So let us not make any issue out of a difference between loving and being loved here.

What this love principally is meant to bring about is the charitable inclination of our heart, and on this we must concentrate now. For our heart has no desire, initially, except to take care of itself, and this desire is to be inverted.

When we first become aware that we do have something that we can describe as a heart, we prefer not to think about it because right away there is a strange and unique sense of responsibility which may or may not coincide with our upbringing. We feel urged to pay attention to various forces and energies and we suspect a very useful application of these.

On the other hand, our individual independence is being challenged, and no one can be expected to go out of his way in order to embrace what seems like less freedom. Freedom, after all, is our most heart-felt hope. We live and breathe for the freedom we hope to achieve and to receive; only that it looks like freedom from want, freedom from fear and insecurity, and so on. Now suddenly we are led to suspect that the pursuit of these individual freedoms makes no real difference to our state, but that an all embracing freedom is available, but only if we reject at the same time the various claims made by our individual will. We do want particular things, and we fully understand, with the commitment of good health and sound mind, that particular, and even peculiar, being is the essence of all that lives, but we have no way of reducing the pressure of all this particularity on our sense apparatus, and so we give up trying to deal with sensation as such altogether and concentrate instead on the impulses created around us in terms of phenomena and of illusion.

The most usual and forthright conclusion to which one leaps here is that of the total relativity of all that matters and of all that can be of interest. Nothing, we decide, is true in itself, but only insofar as it happens to be true for someone or in some relation, and this, after all, is not a bad start, because it removes us from the worship of idols and from the intransigence of false objectivity. Soon, however, we have to admit that this total relativity rounds itself off quite self-sufficiently without in the least taking account of our own hopes and despairs. It leaves us as wretched and as exposed to empty existence as though we had made no headway at all.

We should take this as an encouraging sign, because it can only mean that there is something in us in itself, and if there were not, we should find the system of total relativity relatively satisfactory, as indeed many do.

The need to express current experience recurs therefore. We question the usefulness of experience as such, but only because we have gained the ability to shut ourselves off from it. Love as a voluntary act still makes no sense to us and we refuse to recognize it in circumstances that shut us in and repress our faculties. A little wisdom here goes a long, long way. We notice it in some children, whose unwillingness to be inhibited by us testifies, apparently, to an inhibition in themselves that suits them much better. But all the envy in the world cannot help us to imitate them in this. It would take, again, an understanding born of humility. While we insist that we know better because we have been around longer we run into problems that thwart our best undertakings and frustrate our kindliest ambitions. The experience we seek – and we do seek some sort of a particular experience, let's admit it – must at the same time meet, in us, with the willingness to hand on something of value to others like ourselves. This is an interesting and often exciting stage in contemporary developments. It reassures us to learn that we can be of service, and the understanding that we must be of service if we are to receive what we want often does little to dampen our enthusiasm, and this is only just. Only imagine how rapidly we would forget every good thing that had ever happened to us if we had to depend on a fit into a pre-calculated picture before we went on to the next moment. Consequently we are only too glad to see the sense in the old adage that the life we give makes room for the greater life we receive. The element of death in this should not be overly stressed because we have no way of judging to any worthwhile degree the life of another person.

Or again, it could be maintained that the dogmatic approach to life has greater promise of success because, in a sense, it makes up minds before they can make mistakes, but here we run into the problem of an openness to experience as such. The essential business of what to do when unknown reality appears is well served only by our willingness to let go of any previous conceptions, especially conceptions of love, and to rely entirely on the love that limits and inhibits, so that we are that love, which is after all one of the eight ways the advent of love may bring about.

Instead of getting this love under our control, by which we make ourselves inaccessible to it, we invest that strength in trust, by trusting that this love can in fact do what it is made for.

So it is a fact, first of all, that this love is there, which cannot be stated more precisely, and then we supply the trust, partially so that we do not try to get this love under our control, and entirely so that we may love as much and as well as we are loved. The differentiation into active and passive, again, has to do with a mental operation external to that love and can be recognized as such.

The first thing that this love brings about therefore is its return. We ourselves cannot initiate it. Once we trust it, for which trust we may take the full credit, we are gradually taken up into it until we may say that we love even as we are loved, and here such a thing as the instigation of a process is irrelevant; that is to say, there is neither reason nor use to keep it in mind.

The trust we mean is informed, not blind. If it were blind it would lead to zeal and then to forms of hysteria. But informed trust brings our intelligence to bear on what we feel by choice. Choice feeling is incomparable.

We find it remarkable that so much is done in the name of feeling that would really need this ordinary personality added to it somehow before one could call it credible. But personality in general would account for nothing. How could we limit ourselves from without while at the same time hoping to regulate the very terminology by which our intelligence proceeds? By degrees we approach the fathomable mysteries until clarity is our lot. Fantasy is of ultimate value as a limit of distinction. The perception of fantastic quanta itself holds up the indiscriminate progress of mental or bodily activity long enough for problems to be created ready for solution. An energetic postulate may be presented, for example, as a test case, by which daily incidents may be measured and estimated. Formula succeeds formula as the intellect settles down into a permanent context of love.

When the intellect operates in a context of love it leaves nothing to chance. The love of goodness consumes it and renders its every action fertile. By the same token does the will fail to commit itself except where this love participates. The will is locked to this love. Therefore we may do as we please. Love rules us. We have nothing to fear and we confess to be less than this love even though it uplift us above all else.

57

The central purpose of this love is to create us all equal with respect to goodness and to show us therefore how to do good for one another.

How can we do good for one another? We must first of all recognize one another. This means being able and willing to look through and past our various disguises, both intentional and accidental and it means being able to act entirely on the basis of the personal truth. But the personal truth itself, however we view it, cannot be taken for granted from one moment to the next, and so we are faced with the need for recreating our consciousness of it for the sake of the person near us. This person probably does not think about life the way we do, especially not at that particular moment, so we must limit our search for the personal truth to his nearness, and this limitation is brought about by the love we trust. We could never do it in terms of thought or of feeling alone.

Knowledge of someone's nearness prepares us in a technical way for what that person has to offer, even though that person may not know himself what he has to offer. Then, when we understand what we come to know, we create the opportunity for that person to come to know the same thing. The understanding however must be inhibited by particulars, by the circumstances, for example, in which that person finds himself, both physical and mental; by the time she has and by the time she thinks she has; by the weather, if you like. These particulars appear to the love we trust and are inhibited by it just as it inhibits the particulars of our own personal approach. In a sense you might say that this love also renders us harmless. It effectively modifies the feeble aspects of our character. But it cannot do this, we must remind ourselves, unless we show a willingness to do work, which means we must demonstrate our capacity for eternal life. Such a demonstration requires no special trappings and the time for it is always ripe. In fact we may say that the time is always over-ripe for it, which explains the slight reluctance with which one returns after having slipped into states of partial involvement.

The work we finally do then is eternal even in character, so that the inhibitions and limitations of this love we trust may be viewed in themselves, insofar as they affect us during our work, as stimulants and as access material. This opens up an entirely new realm of inquiry.

We assume that we can go ahead and do something good without interfering with what has already been done, and this, being a free consideration, contributes to the honesty with which we face our circumstances and the conditions under which we work. We cannot, for example, expect these conditions to be favourable, and if we do, we prejudice our efforts and cause ourselves a lot of trouble for nothing. The search for a motivation is of this nature, and we mention it here because the present enquiry would seem to encourage such a search. While we are endowed with an awareness of our various capacities however, we do well to concentrate solely on the concrete aspect of our action and let the rest take care of itself, as it invariably will.

What we must clarify and insist upon at this juncture is the lack of a denominator common to both the good deed and ordinary social behaviour. When people relate to one another in their own interest they have nothing to fear as far as their consciences are concerned and since this is what their activity amounts to, a safe bet, they cannot be faulted. Nor should anyone wish to fault them, since the awareness is lacking and it cannot be improvised. Given this awareness however, in response, usually, to any selfless love, we move out of the system of private and popular motivations and restraints and we begin to concern ourselves with what is good. Even this concern can be said to be good, although it will demand the creation of an appetite for goodness eventually, and the appetite will culminate in the product which will give satisfaction. There is no reason under the sun why we should to be able to speak about it in these terms.

The good deed does not end in a vacuum but it brings about a good thing. There is no need to specify what the good thing is before the good deed is done, and in fact the coordinates are loose, but we will have evidence of something brought about. The point is that we shall not be able to point it out to one another. It exists in eternal terms and this implies a comparative incomprehensibility. It does not imply an incomprehensibility as such, however, and this mistake has all too often been made in the past.

So we may say that our good deeds transport us into the realm of eternal ends. In this realm it is love, and in particular the love that limits and inhibits, which throws light on these eternal ends, allowing us to familiarize ourselves with them and to learn to take them for granted.

Naturally we must first believe that good can be done, and that there is such a thing as goodness, this goes without saying. Finally this belief is subsumed by love. From obedience to faith is a step and from faith to this love is a good deed.

To love, therefore, in the way we would have it here, is to accept all inhibitions and limitations as characteristic opportunities of this love and consequently to take these opportunities in whatever way we may.

The recognition of limitations and inhibitions as such is important, so that we do not confuse them for ourselves, but there is no need to study them, to analyze them or to name or label them. A limitation, as we know, allows for direction, while an inhibition makes for attraction. In the case of a limitation, therefore, we may depend on it to give us direction, while the particular aim for that direction is supplied by us. In the case of an inhibition, we may, similarly, depend on it to make for attraction for us, while the particular source of that attraction is supplied by us.

In the present case before us, for example, we may recognize the limitation of our intelligence, it makes no difference by what, and we choose not to ignore or supersede that limitation in some misguided attempt to improve our freedom but to make it work for us, assuming only that the limitation itself is effectively trustworthy. This assumption is of course basic to the entire process and anyone in the habit of concern over his rights will find nothing to suit him in this. He will prejudge the content of intelligence or else deny outright its form. Then he will go on to make a virtue out of a lack, and so on, until a new set of limitations throws him back further than he imagined himself to be in the first place.

Instead we trust these limitations of our intelligence, and insofar as we have so far trusted them we may see in retrospect the direction we were given and the direction we took. The particular aim throughout is knowledge for the understanding of the elements, which in this case concentrates on the advent of love that limits and inhibits, for a purpose and so as to bring something about. The particular aim here is the distinction of the direction we took from the direction, or non-direction, one might have taken, had one insisted on one's rights rather than trusted in the loving inhibition of one's intelligence. As our description at the moment runs, it should be incidentally clear, and then of its own accord helpfully explanatory, that we may indulge ourselves in aimless directions if we choose wrongly, but there is no such thing possible as a directionless aim.

Reason, we may observe here, becomes conscious of itself at its apex even as it becomes one with love. Consequently it does and exemplifies all in one. This loving reason has no peer and may be envisioned, as the mistress of goodness, or comprehended, as true greatness in action.

The inhibition, at this moment, which makes for the attraction, the source of which attraction we intend to supply, has to do with our capacity for love insofar as we desire that it increase. The source of the inhibition seems to lie somewhere in the realm of our tastes and appetites, where we perceive, on application of our senses, an opulence of beautiful entities on the brink of authoritative expression. The authority interests us insofar as we take it for granted, while the expression is automatically worked in, or allowed to work itself into, the various points of reference under consideration right here and now. The opulence, by no means felt yet, is given a point of departure so that beauty has no need of even a tentative abstraction from the entities to which it relates so perfectly. Consequently their expression follows, as a matter of course and in due course, which is to be preferred even to a connatural behaviour of beings in terms of content and form.

The increase of our capacity for love therefore is achieved in an exercise of loving reason, while feeling is not responsive or not yet responsive, and while our sensation reflects nothing, or nothing yet, that pleases or satisfies us.

Eventually there is an impulse which can only be described as glorious. It goes into experience to the extent of our real adoration. It works true knowledge in whatever way we apply ourselves. It makes it both possible and easy for us to love the light in utter darkness, the word in utter silence, the way in utter confusion, the life in the midst of death and the truth even in falsehood.

*

Next we come to the love that leads. It demonstrates authority because we perceive what we love in the light of external circumstances, which is to say reflectively. Due to the fact that it is we who love, there is an energy we may recognize and an initiative for which we may feel responsible. Due, in truth, to the fact that we are loved, we may agree with ready sensation and elevate that sensation to the level of sober experience.

Love leads, first of all, out of obscurity and into clarity. We value clarity, not for its own sake, but because it allows us to see the truth, the life, etc. for which there can be no other name. But obscurity too has its value insofar as it allows us to grow and to flourish. When we do not see the truth we may desire to be in touch with it, and for this to succeed, clarity is not essential. But since false illusion, delusion in short, would essentially remove us from our desired object, we are aided as it were by a shroud of obscurity, against which we need not struggle. In the authority that is ours we may be certain to understand that this is so; that clarity is not to be achieved at the expense of growth, but that it has its applicability; that we should not cling to it as though we should perish without I; that we should not identify with phenomena.

Then, too, love leads away from terror towards peace. Here the same fact holds, grounded in demonstrable authority. Peace is no end in itself; neither has terror only negative attributes, as we have shown in our philosophy. It is terror that saves us from utter forgetfulness, from the loss of our faculties in distance or in tension. The good service of love removes us from terror when its task is completed, so that we have no cause to fear terror itself, since peace is on the way. Peace is to be desired above all because it finishes all our ambitions in rest, but again, we should not cling to it, while the certainty borne of authority here helps us keep this in mind.

The antithesis mentioned here, of clarity and obscurity, peace and terror, could be multiplied infinitely, and it remains for us to draw the lesson of love, to concentrate on it and to allow its emphasis when opposites in themselves cause us disappointment or involve us optimistically.

Finally we can prove conclusively how love leads to an identification with the truth, with the way, etc. and how there its authority comes into its own. The individual person can only be said to exist once such an identification is made. In another statement, we identify ourselves with the truth, the life, etc., and consequently our person is individual. We ourselves are not individual, but our person is. It finally boils down to my realizing that I am a person but that there is more to me than can be defined as personality, precisely on account of my identification with the truth, the word, etc. There is no way for me to sum myself up, as those pretend to do who insist on their individuality, and as I myself felt like doing when an individuality was presented to me, ready made, freely imagined, a copy for me to copy if I desired the reward of identity in itself. Of course we all wish to be quite certain about us being unique, in one way like no one else, and this wish is confirmed for us by our desire to contribute a special incomparable something, urgently and administratively. The other fact, that the truth, the light, etc. is a particular person, and that there is more to him than his personality sums up, cannot help but occur to us initially, and again sooner or later, as an unpalatable attack on our righteousness, on our decent fellow feeling, on our what you like, and immediately we find ourselves led by the love we are discussing, away from shame and into a position of honour and dignity of the sort that helps us courageously to accept this fact. An identity crisis occurs to bring to our attention a false identity, or our identification with a wrong thing. We lose our individuality so that it may accrue to our person. Our personality is removed so that we may seek it in an identification with the truth, the life, etc., which is to say with the person who is these things

His authority is transferred to us, too, through the love we mean. Due to the love we mean we participate in his authority and aid in its exercise. We may have as much personality as he does, but not more. The fact that we have personality stems from him and the make-up of that personality is the same.

My personality is individual and authoritative insofar as I base it on that subtle element of love out of which I have initially gained my assent to god's interest. As my conscience came into existence I learned to value this divine interest and gradually came to concentrate on it consciously as a source of happiness, while other sources of happiness faded into the background or began to play a subsidiary role. This interest, we now know, carried the very particle of individuality on which our personality later on relied, and this particle is understood as resistance against interest in my self. Divine interest arose and came to recognition out of resistance to self-interest. But self-interest and divine interest occurred as simultaneous events inseparable in time, so that out of the stress occasioned by these two was born my authority to act. I could now act for my self or else divinely; in the interest of the divine. While I did not know to identify this divine interest as such, I merely recognized it as a happiness with an eternal taste, as compared to a happiness with a temporary taste which I had come to reject.

The technique we develop for rejecting our self and its interest is nothing very elaborate nor very sophisticated and may very well come to rely entirely on enlightened feeling, so that we feel the self and find it repugnant or loathsome. Attempts to render this technique elaborate or sophisticated are misguided, like the desire to express failure merely so as to continue to be able to avoid success.

Now since the self is the same whether it is mine or yours, I shall find self-interest in you equally repugnant and similarly difficult to deal with, which highlights the uselessness, finally, of criticism, constructive or otherwise, on both counts: because of what it pretends to accomplish and because of what it does not do. It pretends to improve the whole while only applying to a part, which is an injustice, and it does not do what can only be accomplished by our turning towards the truth, the life, etc. in person.

Here is where the illumination of our various faculties originates. We are meant to be free and easy here, out and out masters of the subject we choose, of the object we instruct or entertain. The temptation to saturate our being with wellbeing, of a preordained character, cannot overrule us, and still we need boundless happiness as we find it offered to us unmerited and uncharged. We come up with trust only to eliminate whatever natural or supernatural contrast lacks efficiency and we impose our will only to assimilate matter. Obviously each and every occasion sets its own pace and translates its own physical counterpart, so we never have to work from the general to the particular of from the whole to the part if we desire to do otherwise. The pattern, in other words, may never extend beyond that which makes use of it. How do we know that we are on the right track?

We remain within our authority which is to say: the authority of the moment. Proposals are immediate accepted, assumptions right away carried out. The salient feature of various articles at our disposal automatically stands out and makes itself relevant by choice. The opaque becomes transparent, the lucid obscure.

At the same time we may rely on our understanding to take care of itself. This should frighten only those whose temperament tends habitually to get the better of them. We behave ourselves as perpetually confined to the ignorance of an organic growth stage until such a time as an alternative becomes available, not eager to change our state nor unwilling to remain in it until our time is up. So thoroughly do we persist in this, that anxiety itself is washed away from us and the normative processes of organic evolution are allowed to develop unhindered. We can compare this to the life of an illusion as it passes through the various states of the narrative process, where fantasy is involved and reality is approached in sequences. The definite order in which phenomena appear pertains only to the senses and to their internal structure. The illusion serves to withdraw from every limited thing its accepted meaning and to abstract bodily appearance from model experience for the sake of a lasting concept. The conclusions we draw as we perform vicariously the acts to which the illusion is subjected have the same normative effect on our nerve system, even to the point of anaesthetic persuasion. Fully expended energy, which is meant to restructure our virtual nature, patterns itself on historic movement in such a fashion as remains relatively unfamiliar throughout the performance. Event is strung to event while the imagination supplies the link we require, the most likely and the most pleasing. In the case of our organism, of course, we remain causally detached, while fiction leaves us at liberty as to the emergency of our critical faculties, so that judgment has the precedent principle only in the case of the organic operation. A legitimate probe of circumstances, prior or during the happening, has no meaning, while a less than legitimate attempt would only lead to a confusing upheaval. This is why we speak ourselves loose of these systems of righteousness and set out on courses of active loving as soon as possible before our sensitivity is clouded beyond reparation. Ordinarily the perspicacity we need to get along is of such a complexity that we push its reflections into the distance and reproduce them as pictures, which are often mistakenly trotted out as ideas. During the various activities of love however we perceive normally; while our perception achieves the highest possible standard, possible for us that is, but in all simplicity and modesty. Then, too, we make do when it comes to the influence we might solicit from the flesh, never going beyond the bounds of the accidental. So our organic aids and causations remain nearby, representative if we so desire, and usefully to the point in any case, warranted by the particular.

Loving activity needs no other application. It appoints itself as its own goal and thence radiates an aura of effectiveness which is passable. We may take it for granted and in our eagerness to take stock of situations where this activity has passed we may infringe against the norms of suitability for a while until we learn to leave well enough alone. Soon we learn to concentrate on the activity and to enjoy the results not as results but as successive norms in their own right.

Loving activity is a case of dynamic charity in progress. It has a peculiar strength, and it originates metaphysically. It is instigated by body insofar as our body is capable of reflection. While we adhere to standards of mind, even to charitable standards of mind, this loving activity must remind beyond us and we are bound to misunderstand it, very likely as false motivation or in terms of separate images.

The peculiar strength of this activity may be measured by our ability to overcome by it whatever threatens our peace and security and it may be experienced as it leads to eternal work. We call it peculiar because it stems from our own characteristic final and unalterable physical being, where matter and form are one and the same. As such it also points to that in us, by derivation, which carries our eternal name and which we mean when we refer to the first personal pronoun singular. This is why we may be known in our works. The peculiar strength of our loving activity treats of the various behavioural aspects beyond which our intellect shall not go without diminishing responsibility. This is very important, especially in the case of an energetic temperament. Our intellect desires responsibility but must disclaim all responsibility that brings it back to itself rather than investing it in reality and in a greater reality. Aspects of behaviour not relevant to a certain personal magnitude are therefore habitually ignored, while those with a leaning to good will are automatically assumed. We may find this confusing, but without losing the thread of the sort of ministerial passivity in which our intellect delights.

The metaphysical origin of loving activity is never beyond the scope of our ordinary enlightened sense apparatus. We say that it is metaphysical merely on account of the fact that in the physical state and process of the activity its origin may not be found, but once we open our intelligence not to the physical alone but to everything, we come into immediate contact with original love, which culminates in loving activity. So far as this original love is concerned, we may obviate our imperfect personality in the face of it, and this gives us a proper indication of where we want to go and what we want to do if we wish to assist in the corporeality of the truth.

The corporeality of the truth is in fact what makes our body capable of reflection and consequently of instigating loving activity. Once again our intelligence is reminded not to lose itself in pictorial displays nor to aid and abet a factitious separation of subjective and objective genera but to exact from the realm germane to itself, from its own proper sphere of freedom, the tender and merciful attributes of existence.

We need hardly emphasize here that tender mercy is the shape of intelligence fully applied. It makes all sacrifice, of any shape or form, superfluous, which is why it may figuratively be called the pure sacrifice. Tender mercy is not an external sign of something interior, nor is anything being destroyed. It could not be, however, unless something once had been destroyed, to wit, our individuality in the truth insofar as it interfered and did combat with the truth, for this our individuality was an internal denial of exterior being and so the abetment of death. Tender mercy is in fact unique insofar as inside and outside have no separate meaning. No signs are therefore involved. It is the most effective activity, being totally effective always. There is no defence against it. If we quarrel with it we quarrel against ourselves and contend self-destructively. To those who hold it in disrepute it will look like falsehood and it will cover them in shame. For this reason it has frequently been ceremonialized. In these ceremonies it is made unusual for the sake of a custom and unapproachable for the sake of an immediate glimpse of it, and of course it requires those who shepherd its eminence through dislocated emotions, past disparate thoughts and opinions, and out again of a network of slight love and meagre charitability. Our own intelligence meanwhile remains in a sort of halfway house, fed but not nourished, beaten but not disciplined, cared for but not really loved.

*

This brings us to the discourse on love that rests in itself and seeks no end outside of itself. It includes all things and embraces all manner of thing. The hope it holds out for those who have never known love is immense and it responds immediately to any request for it. Perhaps we may appreciate this love, as a substance eternally given in which we participate, or else we may undertake to involve it in time, which comes to the same. It resembles the love of the creator for the creature insofar as its main care is natural growth and specific development, but it may be profitably compared to the love of the parent for the child insofar as its motivation can be said to be security and survival.

What we call the cosmos reflects this love in its totality, so that the cosmos is the object of this love. The subject is my own, or your own, which is the same. Subject and object correlate. Their prefect correlation, known and understood, is rest and our energetic being in rest.

We approach the cosmos always anew. It remains equally valid within us and without us. The existence of the cosmos depends on our perception of it, but not the cosmos itself. So we agree that outside of our perception of it the cosmos can neither be said to be nor not to be. The wisdom of this reflects on being itself and prevents the monstrosity. We are or are not only insofar as we perceive, and this is a minimal guarantee of our togetherness. My subject, corelevant to the cosmos, has no meaning outside of itself. If it did, its regress into something like nothingness should exist as a possibility, which is manifest nonsense, but often discussed as though it were not.

We do well, therefore, to distinguish the cosmos from the logos. While the cosmos remains objective and while it exists or not according to our perception of it, the logos is whether we

70

perceive it or not and it is always in a way, in one way or another. We may for example, differentiate between what the cosmos is and what we call it, or what we say it is. In this way the logos impinges upon the cosmos.

The logos, as we just mentioned, always evolves as meaning. The cosmos, in comparison, means what we say it means or what it is said to mean. The cosmos intelligently perceived is a case of the logos meaning it: intelligence is of the essence. We may have an image of the cosmos which lasts in time, for a time, and we may deal with this image logically, which nourishes our senses and entertains our faculties. But an image of the logos would always contain a contradiction in terms. Therefore we subject our understanding to the logos, in order to bring it out of confusion.

Here we come to the point of extraction which must be dealt with separately.

The entire question after beginnings should be seen as a point of order, not lifted out of context and made to carry the burden of infinity as though it were its nature to carry such a burden. We do, after all, ask for a beginning in time only until such a time as we become conscious to the request for a beginning of time itself.

Therefore the logos, without beginning, and the cosmos as the beginning of the logos in time. Memory always regenerates for our purposes the types of past we require, and these purposes serve the one grand purpose of the logos becoming one with the cosmos. Memory must be understood as the operation which regenerates personal experience, of the cosmos and in the logos, for the sake of infinite world, which is cosmos and logos become one.

Since the logos had no beginning, it appeals most strongly to our imagination, just as the cosmos, to the extent that it may be distinguished from the logos, impresses our senses and renders them fruitful.

But just as memory in operation regenerates, so does the intelligent imagination create, and we should never try to see both of these simultaneously or attempt to force them into one category or under one concept. The logos and the cosmos, for example – and this must remain the overriding example for all time – cannot be fully understood and appreciated each in its own right until they have become one, just as a man and a woman who become one are only then fully he himself and she herself. One may say that they represent in their union, which includes the sexual aspect of creation, the union of the logos and the cosmos, but this would lead us too far afield here. Suffice it here to emphasize that when two become one they become fully themselves and that the cosmos and the logos are the example of this.

The cosmos, finally, is the sum total of all conceivable ends just as the logos eventually, is sufficient unto itself. If we relate our various urges and strivings to this we make contact with a visual entity beyond which our faculty of vision will not go but it returns upon itself. This helps us to distinguish between reality and fiction. Fiction depends increasingly on our faculties while its dependence on us diminishes. With reality the opposite is the case. We know that we have what it takes to do and to make things, be it meditation or mud pies. But we must be careful not to differentiate between task and tool except during periods of reflection, and the supreme period of reflection is when vision, the wonderful mistress of all of our faculties, returns upon itself and seals itself in quietness. Now the task is happiness and the tool is our heart. Even as we differentiate we become aware that the two are one, and this may be called the supreme insight. From unity through duality to the oneness of two: this is the shape of the element. For every shape there is a pattern. The various elements of history as such dictate that a man behaves in a way confirmable, if not justifiable, by that from which his behaviour stemmed. If he leans towards a theoretical conception of life, he may be ordained systematically, with special help to keep him in touch with what he sees. If a man's soul is pierced by his own action every time he anticipates beyond the here and now, he may also confer unto others the right to favour or to detest.

A pattern of time has no particular elements by which it may be determined. But a shape as such contains an increment of fatality by which it is directed or attracted. So, as we view contemporary life in progress, our awareness of pattern is conjoined with our passive or active impression of shape and what results is world. We may say that this is how the world, not this world, is created, and eventually sustained.

Pattern contains the two elements of hold and obligation. What we hold is imagined or felt, and similarly do we seek some obligation to sanction necessary performances of our will. We say, for example, that we hold something dear or that we hold it in contempt, and at the same time we urge one another to persist in some behaviour because of a promise, say, or a hope of reward. Pattern combines these two, and our intellect narrows a pattern down, perhaps, to a law or a rule, always as though these could be observed or dealt with by themselves, separate from a body of sense or of knowledge, though we know that they cannot. The particular instance for which the pattern exists, at whatever point we care to view it, must first be offered before the pattern becomes distinct. We need the pattern, as we observe, so that the particular instance may take hold, or we continue to circle in hypothetical frames of reference. But we should not hold on to the pattern. Neither are we obliged to remain in its shadow or afterglow. If we do, we soon develop fixations, emotional possessiveness, addiction to repetition and analysis, etc. We need to be shocked out of these if we are to retain or regain our equilibrium.

Shape, by comparison, eludes our grasp right from the start unless we are willing to wait for the fullness of time with respect to some personal reality. The three elements here are patience, I or you, and the material universe. The last of these may present a difficulty to those of us who are not accustomed to thinking without the aid of derivatives, or to feeling on no basis of recalled experience. The material universe, preferably viewed in its infinite extension, lends itself readily to manipulation on the practical level as long as we make no attempt to devalue its usefulness or to exaggerate aspects of it to corroborate faults in our character. Otherwise the material universe may be said to incline to our wishes. You know this is so due to its evolvement in accordance with our developing intellect. Usually the initial discovery of this accordance confuses us because we have not yet trained ourselves to keep distinct what we may do from what we may be. Then, with training and discipline, we can make the distinction work for us, as the model of discovery and as the mode of invention. You are constantly restrained within all discernible conditions and you persevere gladly under this restrain. You feel entirely alone with me and from this you draw concentration and strength.

The ambition, then, is to limit our experience, not by a set of rules, but in line with some pre-existent whole with which we are hopefully acquainted. There, in patience, we hold out. The fact that we do so willingly, under absolutely no constraint, is of the essence. We are able to distinguish between shape and pattern throughout, but only in hindsight and peripherally. The pattern assumes for us cogent reminders of our mental framework. It stimulates our sense of purpose, weakly and intermittently at first, by encouraging us to look to those various refuges where we hope to avoid what is good and fitting for us. It lines up, in accordance with sensations and thought processes, our inner emotional anxieties and outward defences and offences, so that we may recollect ourselves and find ourselves in a superior order. Without such an order we reach for dissipation and long for disappointment without knowing it.

And the consequence is success. If we believe in the reality of this success rather than taking it on account, subjectively or objectively, subconsciously or hypothetically, we may do works that precipitate this success in one another. Should it not seem likely that the end of transcending achievement is concrete success? For we grow as far as death cannot reach and the justice of our heart mediates in the world, to the benefit of the world, and much sensation springs from our practice of such work. The truth lies before us like human being and human being is available to us as the spring of life, to which we apply our senses and the stream fills us. This is the stream of our passion, that love tempts us to goodness and our deeds hold us in love, fairly prospering in the living we make, in conjunction with the life we live.

This is the end of this science of the elements.

\* \* \*

www.ingramcontent.com/pod-product-compliance
Lightning Source LLC
Chambersburg PA
CBHW070301290526
45791CB00003B/1037